# TAMING

# THE

# TONGUE

## HOW THE GOSPEL
## TRANSFORMS
## OUR TALK

JEFF ROBINSON

FOREWORD I ... IPP

D1004711

Taming the Tongue: How the Gospel Transforms Our Talk
Copyright © 2021 by The Gospel Coalition

Published by The Gospel Coalition

The Gospel Coalition
P.O. Box 170346
Austin, Texas 78717

All rights reserved. No part of this publication may be reproduced, stored in a retrieval system, or transmitted in any form by any means, electronic, mechanical, photocopy, recording, or otherwise, without the prior permission of the publisher, except as provided for by USA copyright law.

Cover design: Gabriel Reyes-Ordeix
Typesetting: Ryan Leichty

Unless otherwise indicated, Scripture quotations are from the ESV® Bible (The Holy Bible, English Standard Version®), copyright © 2001 by Crossway, a publishing ministry of Good News Publishers. Used by permission. All rights reserved.

ISBN:
978-1-7334585-5-9 (paperback)
978-1-7334585-6-6 (ebook)
978-1-7334585-7-3 (kindle)

*Printed in the United States of America*

"Jeff Robinson points us to what it means to be like Jesus, and Christ-likeness is revealed by the way we talk. Robinson's book is steeped in Scripture, full of illuminating examples, and both deeply convicting and also wonderfully encouraging. I am grateful for such a practical and pastoral work and hope that it is read widely."

THOMAS R. SCHREINER, James Buchanan Harrison professor of New Testament interpretation and Biblical Theology, The Southern Baptist Theological Seminary

"This book hit home with me, perhaps because some of my greatest regrets have come from ways I've misused words—confidences I didn't keep, criticism I was too eager to offer, bragging to make myself seem important, dominating the conversation when I should have listened. I've also misused words by keeping silent when I should have come clean, when I should have offered praise, when I should have spoken up. These and many more insights on how we use our words are covered in this brief but wisdom-filled book—a great book to read prayerfully on your own, but even better to use to discuss with a small group."

NANCY GUTHRIE, author and Bible teacher

"Whenever I pick up a book on words or taming the tongue, I brace myself for conviction. It's a struggle I've long known exists for me, and one I fight daily. But it's also one that I find comes back so readily, with new manifestations of its hold in my life. Jeff Robinson has written a book that not only brought the chisel of conviction, but also the hope for transformation. I was convicted of new ways I use my words for evil, but was also reminded of the power of Christ's grace to keep working in me. If you need help taming the tongue (don't we all to some degree?), then this book is for you. I highly recommend it."

COURTNEY REISSIG, author, *Teach Me to Feel* and *Glory in the Ordinary*

"'A word fitly spoken is like apples of gold in a setting of silver.' This striking statement from the book of Proverbs is a potent reminder of how our words can be used to create beauty... or ugliness. Words do indeed have power. Jeff Robinson's study of speech, in both its positive and negative, is an extremely helpful exploration of these realities. May its reading shape the speech of all its readers for the good of their communities and God's glory."

MICHAEL A. G. HAYKIN, professor of church history and biblical spirituality, The Southern Baptist Theological Seminary

"Jeff Robinson offers a compelling treatment of the power of our words to destroy and to heal. If we claim to be his followers, people will judge Jesus by our words and how we speak them. This book contains memorable illustrations, but its greatest strength is its unapologetic appeal to the only words that will last forever: God's."

RANDY ALCORN, author of more than 50 books, and founder of Eternal Perspective Ministries

"With vulnerability and warmth Jeff Robinson shares his own story of taming his tongue. He spurs us on from the Scriptures to consider the power of our words, how we use them, and how the gospel might reshape them for the edification of others. I was convicted, in the best way, in every chapter and ultimately finished the book in awe of God's grace. As one who wields words in my home and in public ministry I will regularly revisit this book."

JEN OSHMAN, author of *Enough About Me: Find Lasting Joy in the Age of Self*

"Some books are about issues unique to our time. Others address matters that relate only to a segment of society, such as men, women, parents, singles, students, expectant moms, those in financial crisis, or another group. But Jeff Robinson's book addresses both a timeless and also universal struggle: taming the tongue. It is full of biblical truth, personal transparency, and practical counsel. If you have a tongue—and an open heart—you'll be both convicted and helped by these words."

DONALD S. WHITNEY, author of *Spiritual Disciplines for the Christian Life* and professor of biblical spirituality, The Southern Baptist Theological Seminary

"Much needed. Highly readable. Constantly applicable. I'll be rereading, passing out copies, and studying with our congregation this book. Why? He addresses the negative use of words without a club; highlights the positive with verve; reminds that good listening lays groundwork for healthy conversations. The book zings with biblical underpinnings, poignant illustrations, and encouraging applications. At times humorous, other times sobering, but always on target, Jeff shows us the effect of living as Christ-followers in our communication. Few subjects could be more strategic than learning how the gospel transforms our talk."

PHIL A. NEWTON, author and senior pastor at South Woods Baptist Church, Memphis, Tennessee

"As Christians, our words are meant to be salt and light, yet we've all uttered words we wish we hadn't—harsh, rash, bitter, unkind, and ungodly. In an age where platforms for quick and careless words abound, *Taming the Tongue* is a timely and much-needed book. With transparency, pastoral care, and biblical truth, Jeff Robinson offers hope for our untamed tongues by pointing us to the one who came to redeem all things—the very Word of God himself."

COURTNEY DOCTOR, coordinator of women's initiatives, The Gospel Coalition, and author of *Steadfast: A Devotional Bible Study on the Book of James* and *From Garden to Glory: A Bible Study on the Bible's Story*

"It is difficult to overestimate the importance that the Word of God places upon our words. The same tongue can destroy and heal. In *Taming the Tongue: How the Gospel Transforms Our Talk*, my friend Jeff Robinson expounds some of the major biblical themes regarding the tongue and applies them with clarity and power. While the book is relatively brief, its brevity does not prevent it from being a clear, illustrative, convicting, but ultimately helpful resource for God's people. The use of memory verses and questions make this book an ideal resource of Bible study or a Sunday school class."

JIM SAVASTIO, senior pastor, Reformed Baptist Church of Louisville, Kentucky

"Since words matter, I'll aim for economy and use, exactly, 15. Astute. Hopeful. Vulnerable. Surgical. Winsome. Timely. Pastoral. Gospel-drenched. Buy it. Read it. You'll love it!"

DAVE HARVEY, president of Great Commission Collective and author of *I Still Do!*

"The social media frenzy we live in now demands a book that reminds us of the power of words to build up or tear down. But imagine if this same book was written by a skilled and clear writer who wrote honestly out of his own pain and harm brought to others through his own careless talk of the past. You hold in your hands such a book! *Taming the Tongue* is that needed book, and Jeff Robinson is that skilled, insightful, refreshingly honest, and transparent author. This needed book is biblically faithful and immensely practical. Every pastor needs to read this book first, for his own soul, and then, to help the souls of those under his care. Every Christian, whether on Twitter or not, will be helped by this book to better learn how to speak words of life and grace to others. No doubt, a providentially timed resource!"

BRIAN CROFT, senior pastor, Auburndale Baptist Church and founder of Practical Shepherding

"No one wants to read a convicting book about taming the tongue, but everyone needs to read this one! Through eye-opening stories and biblical exposition, Jeff Robinson shows the power of one word to ignite wildfires that can consume our relationships, careers, ministries, and more. Jeff's veracious honesty with his struggles creates a safe tone for readers to examine our own. His clear biblical teaching diagnoses the different deformities of sinful speech. And his gospel-saturated approach lifts the drudgery of legalism, inspiring—and even daring us—to tame our tongues, because it is now doable by the grace of God. I highly recommend using this book for personal growth, mentorship, women's ministry, and church-wide readings."

KORI DE LEON, author of *Age of Crowns: Pursing Lives Marked by the Kingdom of God* and director of Adoring Christ Ministries

# CONTENTS

*To my loving, longsuffering wife, Lisa, who has patiently listened to at least 20,000 words per day from my mouth for the past 25 years. Thank you for being graciously frank that day I asked you if I talked too much. The Lord has used that and hundreds of other conversations between us to change me profoundly.*

# FOREWORD

PAUL DAVID TRIPP

It has been so much fun to watch; we have felt so privileged. We have two granddaughters, and we have been with them in those early formative years as they progressed from toddler gibberish to actually being able to communicate with us in real human language. The process is wonderful, mysterious, and holy. They have no idea of the significance of what they are struggling to master. They have no idea that this godlike ability separates them from all the rest of God's creatures. They have no idea how words will form into concepts and coalesce and become a life-shaping worldview. They have no idea how words will shape every relationship in their life. They don't know that they will use words to educate, but also to shame. To love, but also to hate. To serve, but also to demand. To encourage, but also to threaten. To motivate, but also to dominate. To express humility, but also to display pride. They have no idea of the power that has been given them simply because God has entrusted to them the ability to speak. They have no idea that their words will indicate again and again how much they need to be rescued by God's grace. They just want to be able to communicate what they want or what they think they need, but have little understanding of the unique humanity and holiness of words.

But there is something else my dear little granddaughters don't know. It's captured in 10 brief words at the end of Luke 6:45, but it may be one of the Bible's deepest, most profound and spiritually practical statements about how human beings operate: "Out of the abundance of the heart his mouth speaks." It's one of those statements by Jesus that you could quickly read and move on to the rest of your Bible reading for that day, without stopping to reflect on the importance of what those 10 words capture. Jesus is in the midst of explaining how human beings function—that is, why we choose what we choose and do what we do. He directs our understanding of human motivation back to one source, the heart, and his premier example of the inescapable influence of the heart on our functioning is our talk.

You see, the significance—the unique humanity and holiness of our talk—is not just that God gave us this ability, and in that way we are like him. More importantly, this ability is inextricably attached to the causal core of our personhood, the heart. Nothing more centrally defines who we are and why we do everything than the heart does. The heart controls all of our actions, reactions, and interactions, from the smallest, most inconsequential to the biggest, most dramatic, life-shaping decisions.

Words matter because they flow out of our hearts. Communication matters because what the heart is and what the heart does matters. My granddaughters are years from understanding the weighty value of words. They are far from understanding that their words are always heart-revealing. They have no understanding whatsoever that the struggle of words is not a struggle of the right vocabulary, but rather, a struggle of the right heart. They are using more and more words, but they simply have no clue of the life-shaping power of the gift the Creator has given them.

It's important to understand what Jesus is saying: our words do what our hearts have already done. Our words have power and value because everything the heart does has holy value in the eyes of the One who entrusted us with this ability.

The heart *thinks*, and our words are the way those thoughts get communicated and transferred to God and others.

The heart *desires*, and our words are the way we communicate what, how, why, when, and where we want the things that our hearts have come to desire.

The heart *loves*, and every day the loves of our hearts get intentionally or unintentionally communicated to God and to those near us.

The heart *worships*, and our words reveal what rules our hearts.

Words matter because the heart matters. This is why I am so appreciative of *Taming the Tongue*. I have spent the last two decades thinking about words, endeavoring to put my best words down on the page and seeking to speak words of grace wherever God gives me opportunity. But I still struggle to do with my words only what God intended. You are now about to read a book about words that is filled with words of humility, wisdom, warning, and grace. I wish I could say that I don't need this book, but I still do, and I'm sure you do too. What Jeff Robinson has written is not only deep in its understanding of this powerful human ability, but also personally insightful and convicting. Here is ancient wisdom coupled with contemporary application, both of which we all need.

I'll talk today. Sometimes my words will be words of wisdom, love, hope, and grace, but not always. And this is why I still need this book. You'll talk too, and until you're on the other side, your words will also be mixed in intention and vocabulary. So I commend this book to you. May the wisdom here be used of God to season your words with love for him and love for others, so that what you say will give grace to those who hear.

Paul David Tripp

# WHY
# I WROTE A BOOK
# ABOUT TALK

It was an unusual time for one of my elders to request a meeting with me, the senior pastor. It was Saturday, but I wasn't preaching the next day, so I didn't think much about why he wanted to meet. As it turns out, the conversation may have been the most earth-shaking hour I have spent listening to another man in my entire adult life.

My fellow elder was in a deeply serious frame of mind when we sat down. Instantly, the overwhelming thought—paranoia endemic among pastors—entered my mind: *I'm not going to like this.*

My intuition was correct.

He placed a yellow legal pad between us—the front page detailed his concern about me, written in black ink. "I've been watching you closely during your first few months of ministry here, and I've had a number of people in the church come to me about a pretty major issue with you, one I'm pretty sure you're not aware of—it's one I've seen myself."

His tone grew increasingly gentle, telling me this brother wasn't angry with me, but was deeply concerned.

My mind went into overdrive. I frantically replayed parts of the tape of my life during the several months I had served as pastor in this church, searching for clips that would reveal unwitting immorality or moments of extremely poor judgment. Did he think I was involved in some secret sin? Were rumors circulating through the congregation of which I was unaware?

He continued.

"I want you to know that I love you as a dear brother in the Lord. I think you have great potential in the ministry, but you have this one blind spot, and if you don't get ahold of it, you won't be in ministry long."

My mouth was getting dry, and I began to feel my hands tremble slightly. "Okay, I'm listening," I said. "Please tell me what it is."

I wasn't going to like this. My inner attorney rose to his feet, preparing his defense.

"Please know I say this in love from a much older minister to a younger," the elder said.

"Okay, hit me," I said, wanting to get it over with.

"You talk too much," he said. "I mean, you really, really talk too much. You talk about yourself all the time—what you know, what you think, who you know, what you like, what you've done, what you want to do. But you don't listen, and you barely let other people talk. So many words come out of your mouth, it has intimidated some of our members, and they don't want to talk to you, because they know it's just going to be a monologue or a lecture. I realize you're an extrovert and you tend to process things by talking through them, so that makes this hard. Has anyone ever told you this?"

That I was both stunned and stung by his critique is a vast understatement.

"No, I don't think I've ever heard that from another person," I said sheepishly. "I've been teased by friends over being a big talker, but I've never been told it's a huge problem. I need to go away and give this some thought."

After a few assurances that he loved me and that his criticism was an effort to spare me significant relational and ministerial hardship, we parted ways. I wasn't talking anymore, I was assessing. My inner attorney sat back down.

I drove home in stunned silence, not turning on the radio even though it was college football season, and I would normally be dialing in some SEC game. *Could it be true? Wasn't he just being mean? I'm an extrovert, and he and our church members are introverts*, I thought.

As I came through the door, my wife read my shocked face, now probably a little pale. "Are you okay?" she asked. "What was that all about? You weren't gone long."

We sat alone on our front porch, away from the kids, where I recounted our dialogue. Finally, I summoned the courage to ask the person who knows me best: "Is his assessment of my talking correct? Please tell me and don't hold back. If I'm in sin, then I don't need any mollycoddling."

My wife loves me too much to tell me anything but the truth. She took a few seconds to gather her thoughts and she began to speak—slowly and carefully. My first thought was, *I probably don't do what she just did when I'm asked a question. I probably plow ahead.*

"Yes, there is a lot of truth in what he's told you. I've not heard church members say anything about it, but I can see why they might feel that way. I think you need to take his words seriously. Maybe it's not that you talk too much, but it's what you say when you're talking. Sometimes that's what gets you in trouble."

Hundreds of hours in prayer and reflection on Scripture led me to agree with my dear brother and my loving wife. It led to deep self-examination, which exposed layers of sin, self-centeredness, anger, arrogance, pride, and many other unsanctified things in my words.

There was trouble in my talk, and God loved me enough to expose it.

## DELUGE OF WORDS

God's Word is full of, well, words. The Bible's storyline begins with its protagonist uttering the first recorded words in history: "Let there be light."

Those words brought light into being. Over those first six days, God spoke words, and all of creation came into being. The lesson for us: words—particularly God's words—possess incredible power. But human speech possesses a profound power as well—power for life, power for death. No, I don't mean power in words as teachers of the false "name it, claim it" gospel often assert.

The timeline of history is dotted with seismic words. Adam and Eve, our first parents, spoke in the garden. The serpent spoke. God spoke. Our Lord's opponents spoke ("Crucify him!"). Think of history outside the Bible. Think of Augustine and the words of children singing near his garden in Milan ("Take up and read"), Luther ("Here I stand..."), Lincoln ("Four score and seven years ago..."), MLK ("I have a dream..."), Reagan ("Mr. Gorbachev, tear down this wall"). Encouraging words. Inspiring words. Revolutionary words. And, thanks to the words "Did God really say?" there are also terrible, destructive words.

We are a communicating people. Talking heads on CNN, Fox News, and ESPN prattle ceaselessly, analyzing the day's events and issues, many of them trivial—from batting averages to Hollywood hairstyles. Enough books are published each month to sink Noah's ark. And *we talk*. We talk to our spouses, our children, our co-workers; sometimes we talk to ourselves. Using our keyboards and smartphones, we talk on Twitter and Facebook and Instagram. We send text messages and email. All of them contain words.

The conversation is endless. It's been estimated that the average human being utters between 10,000 and 20,000 words per day. Consider that fact in light of Solomon's words in Proverbs 10:19: "When words are many, transgression is not lacking, but whoever restrains his lips is prudent." If the average person speaks between 10,000 and 20,000 words each day, then we are looking at 10,000 to 20,000 opportunities to sin. We all have different temperaments—some of us talk all the time, others not so much—but we all talk, so the Bible and all its talk about talk confronts us.

## NOT THE WAY WE'RE SUPPOSED TO TALK

In the world after Genesis 3, there is trouble in our talk, so how should we use words? Is it okay to vent? To rage? To "tell it like it is"? To use profanity? Words wield incredible power, and the proper and improper deployment of them gets a lot of ink in Scripture. Words begin life-changing relationships: "Will you marry me?" Words start wars: "This day will live in infamy." Words change the world: "He is not here, but is risen from the dead."

Our God is a speaking God who inspired a book to tell us about himself and our relationship to him. Thus, it is important that we develop a biblical theology of words and a practical theology for how we use these deeply powerful tools for the sake of our sanctification, for the sake of the church, for the sake of God's glory.

That's the right place to begin this conversation.

## THREE PURPOSES

This book has three main goals. First, I want to convince readers that words are one of the most important aspects of a life lived before God, one of the best indicators as to our maturation and growth in Christ-likeness.

Second, I want to show how the fall has turned words into potential nuclear warheads, so we must handle them as such.

Third, I want to show how the gospel beats those swords into plowshares and transforms them into conduits of God's grace.

# CHAPTER 1

# GOD'S WORD AND OUR WORDS

*And God said, "Let there be light," and there was light.* (Gen. 1:3)

*You talk too much, you worry me to death, you talk too much, you even worry my pet; you just talk, talk too much.* —R&B singer Joe Jones in his 1960 hit "You Talk Too Much"

In the beginning, there were words. Three verses into the Bible, we read the first spoken words in history: "Let there be light" (Gen. 3:1). God spoke, and there was light. God continued to speak, creating everything on earth and in the heavens, speaking them into existence out of nothing in six days. God's words at creation reflected his power as Creator and sovereign Lord over all things.

On the sixth day, God formed man out of the dust of the ground, breathed life into his nostrils, took a rib from him, and created a woman. God made humans in his image, and endowed them with the ability to communicate through words. The first human speech recorded came from the lips of Adam in Genesis 2:23 where he meets his helpmate for the first time: "This at last is bone of my bones and flesh of my flesh; she shall be called Woman, because she was taken out of Man."

It's easy to read the early chapters of Genesis and miss the fact that God came down and spoke to the humans whom he created. He established a relationship with them. He gave them commands and told them how life works best. The infinite and almighty One makes himself knowable and understandable through human language. Isn't that incredible? God is not distant and aloof from his people as he is so often depicted in popular movies and music.

God comes near and uses words to reveal himself and explain everything else to us. Who is God? He tells us. What's wrong with us and our world? God tells us. Where did we come from, and where are we going? God tells us. How can we know him and live in right relationship with God? He tells us. As John Calvin put it, God uses "baby talk" to make himself known to us; that is, he capitulates to our weakness by making himself known through a form of communication we can understand:

> ... as nurses commonly do with infants, God is wont in a measure to "lisp" in speaking to us ... Thus such forms of speaking do not so much express clearly what God is like as accommodate the knowledge of him to our slight capacity. To do this he must descend far beneath his loftiness.[1]

God did this for our first parents, and he does it for us through his Word. He revealed each phase of his work with words. There's a lot bound up in God's lisping. Think about how much God packs into single words in Scripture when he talks about himself. Various words help interpret the character and attributes of God—including sovereignty, holiness, goodness, omniscience, omnipresence, and omnipotence. God is a rock, the sun, a fortress, a shield, a light in dark places, a shepherd, a protector, a prophet, a priest, a king, a father, a judge, a door, a lamb, a master, water, bread, and much more.

And you communicate almost constantly. You talk, presumably to others, but also sometimes to yourself. You send email. You tweet. You post on Facebook or Instagram. You think words, sing words, write words, read words. Words are at the heart of who you are as a person created in the im-

---

1. John Calvin, *Institutes of the Christian Religion*, vol. 1, trans. Ford Lewis Battles (Philadelphia: Westminster, 1960), 1.13.1.

age of a communicating God. And communication is at the heart of God's nature, as John Frames writes: "[God] in his very nature is communicative... He is, among all his other attributes, a speaking God."[2]

Without God's words, we know neither God nor ourselves accurately. In his prologue to the *Institutes of the Christian Religion*, John Calvin famously wrote, "Nearly all the wisdom we possess, that is to say, true and sound wisdom, consists in two parts: the knowledge of God and of ourselves."[3] How do we know God? Because he has spoken to us. My church's confession of faith has this to say about God's Word:

> The Holy Scripture is the only sufficient, certain, and infallible rule of saving knowledge, faith, and obedience. Although the light of nature, and the works of creation and providence do so far manifest the goodness, wisdom, and power of God and his will which is necessary until salvation... Under the name of Holy Scripture, or the Word of God written, are now contained all the books of the Old and New Testament.[4]

Not many of us stop to consider the fundamental importance of words when we're talking or reading or listening. We just do those things. Adam and Eve's ability to communicate made them unique. Animals don't talk (unless they are Satan-possessed serpents or divinely inspired donkeys). Trees don't talk. Rivers don't talk. But God did, and people made in his image do. God set the trajectory for our lives by giving us this ability. Communication is fundamental to who we are as created beings, and God has wisely designed it that way. Paul Tripp points out:

> There is nothing we depend on more than our ability to give and receive communication. In quiet conversation over coffee, in anxious conversation in a busy airport, in defending why we are late for curfew or didn't complete the task at work, we talk. In teaching our children or intervening in an argument, in a lengthy congressional debate or an intense discussion with a friend, people talk. In a good quiet night, in words of

2. John Frame, *The Doctrine of the Word of God: A Theology of Lordship* (Phillipsburg, NJ: P&R, 2010), 42.
3. Calvin, *Institutes*, 1.1.1.
4. *The Baptist Confession of Faith & Baptist Catechism* (Vestavia Hills, AL: Solid Ground Books, 2010), 1.

athletic challenge, in romantic words of love, in words of correction and rebuke, anger and irritation, people talk. In the confusing patter on a railway platform in India, with the voices of children walking home from school in Soweto, people talk. Words direct our existence and relationships. They shape our observations and define our experiences. We really come to know other people through conversation. We want to be alone when we have heard too many words and we feel alone when it has been a while since anyone has spoken to us.[5]

God's communication to us is lovingly designed to address the need of the moment in simple words that can be understood. We know what a judge is. God tells us he's a judge. We know what a shepherd is, and God tells us he's a shepherd. And before he worked, God told us what he was going to do. He talks about what he's doing and what he's done. Then, he interprets it all for us. Really, that's what much of the Old Testament is and what much in the epistles are—God explaining what he's done for his people. Scripture presents God as the great standard for all communication.[6]

## WHERE IT ALL WENT WRONG

In the beginning, words were good. And the ability to communicate with words is a good gift from the hand of God. There was no slander, no deceit, no abusive talk. But, like all the gifts he's given us, many of them began to be grossly misused after the fall. All our trouble began in Genesis 3. There commenced what Tripp rightly calls a war of words.[7] Now we use words in conflict to insult one another, to lie about one another, to curse God, to spread slander and gossip—basically, to destroy one another. Think of World War II and the infamous memo Nazi general Herman Goering wrote to Hitler saying, "We have reached the final solution for the Jewish problem." That 10-word sentence led to the murder of 6 million Jews and perhaps a million more whom the Nazis declared unfit for human society. Ten little words, incalculable in their tragic effect. Sinful words have led to world wars, civil wars, church wars, familial wars, and murder.

---

5. Paul David Tripp, *War of Words: Getting to the Heart of Your Communication Struggles* (Phillipsburg, NJ: P&R, 2000), 13.
6. Ibid., 9.
7. Ibid., 13.

Satan originated the use of words for evil purposes. God had already warned Adam and Eve in Genesis 2 not to eat of the tree of the knowledge of good and evil. Everything is still pristine at this point. Genesis 2 ends on what seems like an odd phrase: "And the man and his wife were both naked and were not ashamed" (Gen. 2:25). Why did God need to point out they were naked and not ashamed? Because shame would soon invade human relationships.

That odd sentence sounds foreboding and sets the stage for the next chapter. The curtain rises on Genesis 3, and the serpent slithers into the garden. He speaks to Eve about God's prohibition that forbids them from eating from the one tree. Satan asks Eve, "Did God really say?" This question sets off a chain reaction of ill-begotten words between the serpent and our first parents that ends with them eating the forbidden fruit.

God speaks to Adam, Eve, the serpent, and the entire created order: "Cursed are you." Ten thousand nuclear warheads exploding every day could never rival the cosmic impact of those words. It's why there's trouble in our talk. It's why Jesus came. Those few words declared in Eden triggered the fall of man from innocence. They opened the door wide for two intruders: sin and death. A few chapters later in Genesis 11—following Noah and the flood—sinful men at Babel use language to reshape reality, "believing and declaring that we are able to bring God down and so de-god God, who is ultimate reality. It is then a short stop from this idolatrous construal to reimagining everything else."[8] In judgment of their self-idolatry, God stopped their work by making their words unintelligible to one another, and he scattered the people across the earth. Filled with secular hubris, human wickedness had grown to such a degree that the people began to mimic the words of God; in Genesis 11 they repeatedly said, "Let us," brazenly seeking to commandeer God's creative power of words and language.

Words, once creating life in a world God called good, now bring death. Human hearts are now idle word factories. In Matthew 12, Jesus says, "You brood of vipers! How can you speak good when you are evil? For out of the abundance of the heart the mouth speaks" (Matt. 12:34). Our heart, now enslaved to sin and death, shows its diabolical way by what comes out of our mouths.

---

8.  Melvin Tinker, *That Hideous Strength: How the West Was Lost* (Welwyn Garden City, UK: Evangelical Press, 2018), 42.

## HOW IT WAS ALL SET RIGHT

The misuse of language at Babel brought God's wrath, but the storyline of Scripture does not stop there. In Acts 2, the Holy Spirit un-confused the languages such that men began to hear the gospel in their native language. The Messiah foreshadowed in Genesis 3:15 crushed the head of the serpent as promised, defeating him at Calvary, dying on the cross and coming out of the ground on the third day. Seismic words tell the story, first at Golgotha, where Jesus bore the wrath for his people's sins: "It is finished" (John 19:30). Three days later, the angel reported to the women at the tomb seven words that changed history: "He is not here. He is risen" (Mark 16:6b).

Forty days after he arose, Jesus ascended into heaven and soon thereafter, the promised Spirit came to indwell God's people. The curse of Babel was reversed. Now, because of Christ's death and resurrection, by the power of the indwelling Holy Spirit, God's people could again use words to build up and not tear down, to give life, rather than bring death. John's Gospel tells us that the Word of God has changed everything:

> In the beginning was the Word, and the Word was with God, and the Word was God. He was in the beginning with God. All things were made through him, and without him was not any thing made that was made. In him was life, and the life was the light of men. The light shines in the darkness, and the darkness has not overcome it. (John 1:1–5)

How does the Word affect our words? One of the most powerful reminders in all of Scripture of the grace we've received and how it should shape our posture—even our talk—toward others is found in Matthew 18:21–35, the parable of the unforgiving servant. The disciples thought they were being charitable when they asked Jesus if we should be willing to forgive those who've wronged us seven times. But Jesus told them we must forgive "seventy times seven" times, which means we must be willing to forgive an infinite number of offenses—seven representing the number of completeness in Scripture. Then, like a great preacher, Jesus illustrated the truth by setting forth two servant debtors—one who owed the king the equivalent of millions of dollars, and one who owed that servant a relatively small amount. The king demanded full payment of the unconscionable debt the servant owed him, but the poor servant begged for more time. Then, inexplicably, the king forgave the debt—entirely. This story powerfully illustrates what

Christ has done for each of us who've come to faith in him: he has paid an infinite debt we owed but could never repay.

But the story doesn't end there.

The servant who'd been forgiven what was virtually an infinite debt then encountered a fellow servant who owed him a small debt. He demands immediate payment, and when the other servant begs for more time, he begins to choke the second servant, demanding, "Pay what you owe." Then the forgiven servant has the other servant cast into prison until he can pay the debt. The king, upon hearing of the forgiven servant's ungracious behavior, has him arrested and jailed until he is able to pay the debt that had been previously canceled.

Jesus delivers the lesson in verse 35: "So also my heavenly Father will do to every one of you, if you do not forgive your brother from your heart."

The lesson as it applies to our communication struggles is this: as the redeemed of God, we have been forgiven an infinite debt. In dealing with others, even in the way we talk to them, we have no right to mistreat them. Jesus demands that we give them grace in the way we treat them and in the way we speak to them. To mistreat another person verbally is to forget that we did not get what our sins deserved, that Jesus paid our debt with his life. This sacrifice should liberate us to speak to others with kindness, humility, and grace. God's indwelling Spirit empowers us to talk graciously to others in ways we never could in our unregenerate state.

## TROUBLED NO MORE

Still, even though we are redeemed, we misuse words. The tongue must still be tamed. We live between the times—the already and the not yet—and our communication is still getting straightened out. We sin with angry words. We sin with lying words. We sin with threatening words. We sin with boastful words. We sin with profane words. We sin with gossip. We sin in conversations, in email, and on social media. Though we are filled with God's Spirit, though we are being transformed day by day into the image of Christ, our communication struggles remain. But, because the gospel is true, we can gradually see our words conformed to Christ.

One day our troublesome talk will be no more. One day Christ will fully consummate his kingdom, death will be dead, sin will be cast into hell, and God's people will live in a kingdom with citizens who communicate with perfection. We rejoice in these words:

Then I saw a new heaven and a new earth, for the first heaven and the first earth had passed away, and the sea was no more. And I saw the holy city, new Jerusalem coming down out of heaven from God, prepared as a bride adorned for her husband. And I heard a loud voice from the throne saying, "Behold, the dwelling place of God is with man. He will dwell with them, and they will be his people, and God himself will be with them as their God. He will wipe away every tear from their eyes, and death shall be no more, neither shall there be mourning, nor crying, nor pain anymore, for the former things have passed away." (Rev. 21:1–4)

But first, we need to see clearly why words are so dangerous and why they must be handled with great care.

## MEMORY VERSE

*In the beginning was the Word, and the Word was with God, and the Word was God.*
(John 1:1)

## QUESTIONS FOR GROUP DISCUSSION

1. Genesis 2 tells us that God made men and women in his own image. The creation account also shows that he is a talking God. How does his talking and communication relate to ours? How is our talk similar and different from his?

2. How many words does the average person use in one day? Does that number surprise you? What might this mean for those among us who tend to talk more than others?

3. What did you spend most of your day talking about today? What topic(s) did you give the most attention to? What do you spend most days talking about?

4. How has the fall in Genesis 3 affected our talk? How does this shape what you talk most about, and how would you like to see that change?

5. In what ways does God describe himself in Scripture, and what does that say about the richness and importance of words?

6. What are three main purposes for this book? What are the areas that cause you the most trouble in your communication with your spouse or

children? Other family members? At work? In church? How do you hope to grow in those areas from this study?

FOR FURTHER READING
AND STUDY

- *War of Words: Getting to the Heart of Your Communication Struggles* (P&R, 2001) by Paul David Tripp
- *The Power of Words and the Wonder of God* (Crossway, 2009) edited by John Piper and Justin Taylor

CHAPTER 2

# TROUBLE IN OUR TALK

*If anyone thinks he is religious and does not bridle his tongue but deceives his heart, this person's religion is worthless. (James 1:26)*

*If the tongue is frequently without a bridle; if it may be observed, that a person often speaks lightly of God and of divine things, proudly of himself, harshly of his fellow creatures; if it can be affirmed with truth, that he is a liar, a talebearer, a railer, a flatterer, or a jester; then whatever other good qualities he may seem to possess, his speech betrayeth him; he deceiveth himself, his religion is vain.* —John Newton[1]

One sentence, one tweet, or even one word spoken the wrong way at the wrong time before the wrong audience—be it one person or deceives—can wreck our lives.

---

1.  John Newton, "Thoughts on the Government of the Tongue" in *The Works of John Newton*, vol. 4 (Carlisle, PA: Banner of Truth, 2015), 588.

There's trouble in our talk.

Just ask John Rocker.

Once a star relief pitcher for the Atlanta Braves, Rocker gave an expletive-and-insult-filled interview to *Sports Illustrated* reporter Jeff Pearlman that came on the heels of an expletive-and insult-filled ride from the airport to the interview venue. Often, arm trouble ruins a pitcher's career. Pearlman's interview more or less sunk Rocker's. Within three years of Pearlman's interview, Rocker was done in MLB, considered a pariah and a potential cancer in the clubhouse. No team would touch him.

Loose lips sink ships. They ruin careers.

Just ask former U.S. President Richard Nixon.

Ever the paranoid leader, Nixon secretly taped every conversation that took place in the Oval Office. The recordings wound up providing investigators with the smoking gun that led to his resignation from our nation's highest office. Nixon's own words proved him guilty of complicity in the Watergate crimes.

The tongue must be tamed.

Just ask Justine Sacco.

One irresponsibly worded, ill-timed tweet—12 words—wrecked her life for months on end in 2013. Sacco, a communications executive with the media company IAC, sent an acerbic tweet to her 170 Twitter followers just before boarding a plane for Africa: The tweet dripped with racial animosity—"Going to Africa. Hope I don't get AIDS. Just kidding. I'm white!" During her 11-hour flight to Cape Town, the tweet spread like wildfire from her tiny band of Twitter followers until Sacco became the number one worldwide trend on Twitter.

Hundreds called for her firing; many called her a racist, a hate-monger, and worse. Her employer made clear via social media that Sacco was "currently unreachable on an intl flight." Sacco's phone was off, and she had no idea that Twitter's tectonic plates were rumbling beneath her account. As Sacco's flight flew the length of African continent, drama built on Twitter about what was going to happen when the plane landed, and she turned on her phone. One Twitter user even went to the airport to take pictures of her upon arrival. To make a long story short, IAC fired Sacco. Social media mobs piled on, and she was shamed and unable to find employment for months. Sacco nearly had a nervous breakdown.[2]

One tweet. Twelve words. Months of shame and misery.

Words have life.

These three cases powerfully illustrate Proverbs 13:3: "Whoever guards his mouth preserves his life; he who opens wise his lips comes to ruin."

The tongue must be tamed.

Just ask Arius and Athanasius.

At the Council of Nicaea in AD 325, heresy and orthodoxy as to the person of Jesus Christ hung, not on a word, but on two Greek letters—a dipthong—in the middle of a word. One combatant in the debate was an early church hero named Athanasius (296–373) from Alexandria. The other major figure was a Libyan priest named Arius (b. 250). Basically, the dispute was whether Jesus was and is *homoousios*—of the same substance with the Father—or was and is *homoiousios*—of similar essence to the Father.

If Jesus is *homoousios*, then it means he is of the same essence of the Father, and thus you have one God in three persons. If Jesus is *homoiousios*, then he's of similar essence to the Father, which means he's separate from the Father, and so Jesus is either another god or a divinely touched man. You see the difference. Athanasius and his party held that Jesus is of the same essence as the Father. Arius and his supporters argued that the true biblical understanding of Jesus is that he is of similar essence with the Father. Arius's infamous teaching on Jesus was that "there was a time when he was not."[3] In other words, he is the first and highest of all created beings. This is what Jehovah's Witnesses today believe.

Words give life, and words bring death—even eternal death. To see the fallout as it pertains to words, let's look at a three places where God's Word instructs us plainly about our speech: a few of many passages from Proverbs, Matthew 12, and James 3. Two things will become clear from examining God's Word: Every time we open our mouths, we are on the cusp of sinning,

2. Jon Ronson, "How One Stupid Tweet Ruined Justine Sacco's Life," *The New York Times Magazine*, February 12, 2015, https://www.nytimes.com/2015/02/15/magazine/how-one-stupid-tweet-ruined-justine-saccos-life.html; accessed September 5, 2019. There are a couple of other powerful stories in this article that show lives ruined from what seemed to be small missteps on social media.

3. For an excellent discussion on the Council of Nicaea, see Nick Needham, *2000 Years of Christ's Power, Volume 1: The Age of the Church Fathers* (Ross-Shire, Scotland: Christian Focus, 2016), 219–49.

and the malignant words that come forth signal the presence of a far more serious cancer.

## PROVERBS: A TREATISE
## ON TALK

God's book of wisdom contrasts the life of the foolish man with the life of the wise man. It shows us how life works best in a fallen world. And talk is deeply important in recognizing which of those two paths we're walking. Paul Tripp even argues that Proverbs is most fundamentally a treatise on talk.[4] He summarizes Proverbs' teaching on talk this way: "words give life; words bring death—you choose."[5] Every utterance that escapes our lips matters, which means you've never spoken a neutral word in your life.

Our words are moving either in a life direction or a death direction. If our words are moving in a life direction, they will be words of encouragement, hope, love, peace, unity, instruction, wisdom, and correction. But the death direction brings forth words of anger, malice, slander, jealousy, gossip, division, contempt, racism, violence, judgment, and condemnation.[6] We don't give much thought to our talk in mundane times, yet that's where we tend to get into trouble, and Proverbs instructs us well.

Proverbs begins with eight chapters establishing the greatness of wisdom, and it personifies wisdom as a good woman who raises her voice in the streets, calling the young man to take her path, the road to the good life. The first place we see words become downright dangerous is in Proverbs 5:3, "For the lips of the forbidden woman drip honey, and her speech is smoother than oil." The forbidden woman is depicted as seeking to lure the man into an adulterous affair, and the bait comes from her lips. When he falls prey to her seductive words, Solomon says he is destroyed, and "his disgrace will not be wiped away" (Prov. 6:33b). Adultery ruins lives, and it usually begins with enticing words.

Proverbs offers an encyclopedia of insights into our talk. Perhaps most sobering is Proverbs 6, which provides a list of the things God finds detest-

---

4.   Paul David Tripp, "War of Words: Getting to the Heart for God's Sake" in John Piper and Justin Taylor, eds., *The Power of Words and the Wonder of God* (Wheaton, IL: Crossway, 2009), 24.

5.   Ibid.

6.   Ibid.

able, seven things he hates: haughty eyes, a lying tongue, hands that shed innocent blood, a heart that devises wicked schemes, feet that are quick to run to evil, a false witness who breathes out lies, and one who sows discord among brothers (Prov. 6:16–19). Of the seven, four relate to communication. "Haughty eyes" refers to an arrogant, nonverbal stance toward others intended to intimidate and demean.[7] A "lying tongue" and "false witness" both refer to deceptive speech and sowing discord among brothers, which uses gossip, slander, or other sinful talk to introduce discord to the church. God hates sinful speech, especially when it introduces chaos into the church for whom his Son died.

Several chapters in Proverbs are rich with wisdom for our communication, particularly chapter 10, where Solomon writes: "When words are many, transgression is not lacking, but whoever restrains his lips is prudent" (Prov. 10:19). Let's face it: some people talk too much. According to the elder who lovingly confronted me a few years ago, I'm one of them. For extroverts and those who get paid to talk (I happen to fall into both categories), this means that 20,000 words (or more) per day means 20,000 opportunities to sin. This is a sobering truth, as Gary Brady points out:

> As sinners, the more we talk, the more likely we are to sin. You say something for a joke; it goes well, so you try something else but it is not funny and hurts people. You are talking late at night, but start to gossip maliciously. You decide you must speak to someone about his actions, but you go too far and say what is untrue. You say something that you hope will provoke a reaction; it falls flat; so you try something more extreme, something wicked.... Moreover, the more we say about ourselves, the more likely we are to boast. It was once said of a long-winded preacher that he preached the congregation into a good spiritual frame and then preached them out of it again. Long prayers can have the same effect.[8]

Look no further than talk radio or cable television for evidence. Pundits drone on and on, 24 hours a day, seven days a week, and there is often little

---

7. Tim Muelhoff, *I Beg to Differ: Navigating Difficult Conversations with Truth and Love* (Downers Grove, IL: IVP, 2014), 21.

8. Gary Brady, *Heavenly Wisdom: Proverbs Simply Explained* (Webster, NY: Evangelical Press, 2003), 271.

substance, much less wisdom, in their talk. Often there's outright sin in the things they say and in the way they say it.

But sinful talk is by no means limited to professional talking heads—it infects us all. James warns those of us who teach the Bible to watch our words carefully. Before launching into one of the Bible's most memorable discussions of our talk, James begins by saying, "Not many of you should become teachers, my brothers, for you know that we who teach will be judged with greater strictness" (James 3:1). Combine that with Proverbs 10:19, and we who handle the things of God for a living need to be doubly cautious in the things we say about God and on behalf of God. Proverbs 10 further contrasts two kinds of talkers—the wise and the foolish:

> The tongue of the righteous is choice silver; the heart of the wicked is of little worth. The lips of the righteous feed many. But fools die for lack of sense. (Prov. 10:20–21)

> The mouth of the righteous brings forth wisdom, but the perverse tongue will be cut off. The lips of the righteous know what is acceptable, but the mouth of the wicked, what is perverse. (Prov. 10:31–32)

Solomon cuts to the heart of what this book is arguing in Proverbs 18:21:

> Death and life are in the power of the tongue, and those who love it will eat its fruits.

In America when police officers arrests a person, they caution him regarding his rights, including the Miranda warning, which begins, "You have the right to remain silent. Anything you say can and will be used against you in the court of law." Words, when uttered by a person accused of committing a crime, can be a matter of life and death, at least when it comes to what could happen during the trial. Say something foolish, and life could become even more difficult for you. So it is in everyday life. Words have the potential to kill and to give life. We all know people (maybe even ourselves) who have been verbally abused by parents, spouses, even friends, to a point that the insults have become part of their identity and have ruined their lives.

In college I had a friend whose father had told him he was stupid for so many years he'd come to believe it and embraced it as central to his identity. His father's constant disapproval, usually shown through verbal jabs, led him to a life of drug and alcohol abuse before college. In a sense, his father's words had killed him. Our words affect others, with the potential to destroy them.

As we will see in chapter four, words can also give life. Think of how encouraging that Christian friend was to you when they told you how skilled you were in something you valued—maybe your singing voice, your teaching ability, your golf swing, how well your children read. Think about how your daughter smiled when you told her how proud you were that she had made the honor roll or all-star team.

Pastors have a special relationship to Monday. We often call it "Blue Monday," because it's the day we spend in recovery mode from the rigors of Sunday and that sermon we spent 15 hours preparing only to see it fall as flat as the Kansas prairie. It's the day that church member emails his pastor to complain about the music or the length of the sermon or how the youth group isn't meeting his family's needs.

I remember one particularly depressing Monday a couple of years ago when I was down and out over what church members had apparently regarded (but didn't notify me) as low attendance Sunday. I'd also learned our giving was way down, and one prominent family had announced to me that they were leaving because they didn't like the elders' vision. "Too much Bible," they told me. I opened my inbox that day, convinced I would only encounter additional ill news, but the first message to appear was from a relatively new member. His words were as humble as they were sweet. He was grateful for our church's faithfulness, for the elders' clear-headed vision, for our church's friendliness. He loved that we valued the Bible enough to make it central to everything we do. The Monday blues were gone. In two short paragraphs, his words breathed new life into my week. I could look up at the mountain peak that was next Sunday with a smile. He had given me what Solomon describes in Proverbs 25:11: "A word fitly spoken is like apples of gold in a setting of silver."

Words kill and words give life—that's what Solomon is saying. The New Testament's answer to Proverbs contains the most sustained discussion of the tongue in the entire Bible.

## JAMES 3: SMALL ORGAN, MASSIVE IMPACT

The *Titanic* was a monster of a ship. It had nine decks, was 175 feet tall from the hull to the top of the highest smoke stack, and weighed more than 46,000 tons. Yet the rudder, which is basically the steering mechanism that guided it through the water, was 15 feet long and appeared frail by comparison. Let that sink in for a moment. Forget that the ship sunk four days into its maiden voyage; that disaster had nothing to do with the rudder. That massive ship was guided by a comparatively tiny instrument, like an ant leading an elephant across the plains of Africa on a leash.

I live in Kentucky, a state famed for horse racing. You won't drive far without seeing a beautiful thoroughbred, or at least a statue of one. Visit Churchill Downs in Louisville for a race, and you'll feel the power of these massive animals as they run past. The ground rumbles and shakes as the horses pass near, hurtling all-out toward the finish line. But the bit at the end of a bridle is just a few inches wide. Jockeys can (usually) steer the horse in any direction they please, even at high speeds, with that small bit attached to the bridle.

James 3 compares the human tongue to a ship's rudder and a horse's bridle. His point is this: in our world, small things often have outsized impact. And that's doubly true for the tongue. After James warns those of us who teach the things of God—and I believe this is the kind of teaching in view in 3:1—he admits that we all stumble in many ways. But if we could only stop sinning with our tongues, if we were able to stop talking sinfully, then we would be sinless and perfect. This is how important our words are and how difficult it is to use them for good. James says it's impossible for the citizen of a post-Genesis 3 world to refrain from sinning in his or her speech.

So if the rudder drives a ship, and the bit allows the jockey to control the horse, the question for us is this: in what direction is our tongue driving us? Toward God or away from him? Every word we use does one or the other. We encourage or we criticize. We teach the Bible or we rhetorically eviscerate our opponent to win a debate. We tell our son to go clean up his room, please, or we tell him he's nothing but a messy fool. When we use our words to establish our will rather than God's, we are courting disaster.[9] I weigh

9.    Timothy S. Lane and Paul David Tripp, *Relationships: A Mess Worth Making* (Greensboro, NC: New Growth Press, 2006), 73.

roughly 190 pounds. Our family doctor told me my tongue probably weighs about 2.5 ounces (I asked him for the purposes of this book), yet it is the steering wheel that often drives the human bus.

The tongue is perhaps the most powerful force that can be unleashed by a human on earth. One application we can already draw from James is this: Christian maturity is, in part, tied to the degree to which we are able to bridle our tongues.[10] Just like a bit and rudder, James says, "So also the tongue is a small member, yet it boasts of great things" (James 3:5).

Charles Spurgeon was nearly driven out his mind and out of ministry by a single ill-timed word. On October 19, 1856, Spurgeon was preaching at the Surrey Garden Music Hall in London. Mid-sermon, a man in a faraway balcony (and out of the preacher's earshot) shouted "Fire!" The entire section fled, stampeding out of the building. Seven were trampled to death, and 21 were left with life-threatening injuries. There was no fire. But one word spoken in the wrong place at the wrong time produced deadly disaster. Spurgeon nearly had a nervous breakdown in wake of the disaster, and he wrangled with anxiety and depression for the rest of his life.

All from one word.

James further fleshes out the trouble in our talk in 3:5–6 where he sketches a picture of the catastrophic damage our talk can cause. He compares the tongue to a raging, destructive forest fire that begins with a small spark that falls into dry leaves or undergrowth. In November 2016, a forest fire swallowed much of the touristy East Tennessee towns of Pigeon Forge and Gatlinburg, Tennessee. At least 14 died, 150 were injured, and more than 2,500 homes and businesses burned to the ground. Thousands of acres were burnt to a crisp. The fire was thought to have begun by teenage boys starting a campfire. A fire that began no more than three or four feet in diameter grew into an unconscionably destructive inferno. Similarly, the fire that burned nearly 500,000 acres in northern California in late 2018 began when a rancher drove a metal stake in the ground in attempt to plug a yellow jacket's nest. One strike created a spark that ignited the grass and, despite his valiant attempts to extinguish the blaze, it grew into a conflagration that destroyed hundreds of homes and took weeks to extinguish.

---

10. Sinclair Ferguson, "The Bit, the Bridle, and the Blessing: An Exposition of James 3:1–12" in John Piper and Justin Taylor, *The Power of Words and the Wonder of God*, 46.

In the same way, James says, "The tongue is a fire, a world of unrighteousness" (6a). Remember what Solomon said in Proverbs? Words kill. They burn down relationships and destroy lives. James goes on to say, "The tongue is set among our members, staining the whole body, setting on fire the entire course of life, and is set on fire by hell" (3:6b). Sinful talk has its origins in hell, and it touches every corner of the life it sins against. Everywhere the tongue makes its presence felt in a sinful way, it leaves a stain that spreads through the person. Perhaps it's a stain only God can see, a defiling mark left on the person—the personality has been stained. The entire course of life changed. Think about how talk altered the paths of John Rocker, Richard Nixon, and Justine Sacco.

Why does James say the tongue is set on fire by hell in James 3:6? Evil words destroy because they come from Satan himself, who is the father of lies. That's his native tongue: "Has God really said?" And think of the lies he told Jesus during our Lord's temptation in the wilderness when he twisted Scripture. Hell even uses our tongue when we mean well with our words—think of Peter's words to Jesus after our Lord told the disciples he was going to Jerusalem to die; Peter said, "This will never happen to you, Lord!" Jesus responded, "Get behind me, Satan! You are a hindrance to me." The ever-clumsy pre-Pentecost Peter unwittingly tried to talk Jesus out of going to the cross. Without question, his words were driven by the Devil.

In James 3:7–12, James points out that every type of animal has been tamed by man, but says no one can tame the tongue. James points out the problem for followers of Christ: we tend to be double-tongued. We go to church on Sunday morning and praise the Lord. Then, on the way home, we complain about the sermon, we slander a fellow church member, or we gossip about a friend. When we do that, we are functioning like a spigot that spews out both salt water and fresh water at the same time. Yes, we may offer words of encouragement to a friend that are like "apples of gold in a setting of silver," but then we criticize that same friend behind their back over some trivial matter or some imagined offense they've committed against us. It's clear that James is addressing Christians because of what he says about our forked tongue in 3:10b: "My brothers, these things ought not to be so."

How will we tame the tongue? We'll begin to see some gospel light toward that end in chapter four. But before we discuss that, we need to see—and feel the jarring effect of—some of the most frightening words in the Bible, particularly for those of us who utter 20,000 words or more every day. Jesus's hard words in Matthew 12:33–37 help us to see what's at stake and why this book is necessary in the first place.

## MATTHEW 12: X-RAY OF THE HEART

In early 2018, my close friend Phil Newton thought he was going to the doctor for a routine annual checkup. No doubt the doctor would tell him that he was healthy, with the promise of a couple of decades more of faithful pastoral ministry. But the doctor found some signs that concerned him. This led to tests and a colonoscopy, which is essentially an X-ray of the colon performed with a camera. This revealed big trouble: Phil had stage four cancer that had spread. On the outside, he looked fine, but on the inside lurked a deadly disease.

Jesus says our tongues are like that. They serve as an X-ray organ that reveals what's going on in our hearts. In Matthew 12, he addressed the Pharisees about good hearts bearing good spiritual fruit and diseased hearts bearing rotten spiritual fruit. Then, in verses 34–35 he says this (and so much for the "gentle, meek, and mild Jesus"):

> You brood of vipers! How can you speak good, when you are evil? For out of the abundance of the heart the mouth speaks. The good person out of his good treasure brings forth good, and the evil person out of his evil treasure brings forth evil.

There is the X-ray. Jesus says the condition of our hearts is evidenced by the words we use. The Greek word the ESV translates as "abundance" literally means "overflow." The words we speak bubble up out of the overflow of our hearts like pouring too much water into a Mason jar. So there is a more fundamental issue here than our words: the heart. What controls the heart will direct the life. What controls the heart will control our words—and our words make visible what is invisible to the naked eye. Our talk issues are really heart issues. Until the heart is changed by God's grace, the talk won't change, and our words won't change. Simply resolving to "do better" with our words won't produce change.

Growing up, my family had an apple tree in our back yard. Each summer, it would produce shiny, red, delicious fruit. One year, brown, mushy apples appeared. The next year, only a few rotten, shriveled apples came forth. What was wrong? The tree's roots were dying. Those bad roots produced bad fruits. We couldn't merely go to the grocery store, buy a few dozen Red Delicious apples, and then staple them to the limbs. That wouldn't have been healthy fruit—not really. The roots were the problem—they were rotten, and they produced rotten fruit. In the same way, our talk won't be healthy until our heart is healthy. That's what Jesus is saying in Matthew 12—the words that come out of our mouths—evil or good—show us the condition of our hearts. If you want your fruit of our communication to be healthy, pray for God to make your heart healthy.

## PAYDAY SOME DAY

Our Lord's solemn words in Matthew 12 should raise all sorts of questions. What comes out of my mouth when I get angry? What do I say when the teenagers are fighting in the car, or my wife is still fixing her hair at nine on Sunday morning, and I'm waiting in the car in the driveway? What about when a fellow elder confronts me about some sin? What about that deacon who asks how long I plan on preaching just before I step into the pulpit? What about when my boss tells me my work on a project was shoddy? Does my inner attorney immediately rise from his seat to defend me? Here's another important diagnostic question: what do I talk mostly about? My spouse? My kids? The Georgia Bulldogs? Myself? Jesus says what I talk about gives a clear picture of what's in my heart.

Then, in verses 36–37, our Lord utters the most sobering part:

> I tell you, on the day of judgment people will give an account for every careless word they speak. For by your words you will be justified, and by your words you will be condemned.

On judgment day, the "day of days," we will give an account for every sinful word. That's staggering. If I average 20,000 words every day and if Solomon is correct that "when words are many, transgression is not lacking," then the possibilities are unconscionable. If I live to celebrate my 80th birthday, then I will have uttered more than 600 million words—with that many opportunities for sin.

Then Jesus says we will be justified or condemned by our words. I don't take that to mean my words spoken at the judgment will tell where my heart lies. And of course, we believe that we are justified by faith and not by works—or words. I think what Jesus is saying is this: Words carelessly spoken are eternally important. The words I've used over the course of my life confirm or deny whether I've truly undergone a heart transformation by God's grace.

Have you ever made a remark to someone and then said, "Oh, I'm sorry, I didn't mean to say that"? But, really, you were being honest when you said it, but you didn't like the way it sounded. Sometimes we do misspeak accidentally. But when we say, "I didn't mean to say that," it actually speaks volumes about the trouble we have with our talk. It gives us an X-ray of our heart.

And Jesus saying "every careless word" is doubly frightening, because much of the time our verbal sins arise in the mundane times when we've let our guard down, and we're just shooting from the hip. I remember once when I was leaving church on a Sunday morning after having preached to the congregation. I was walking to my truck with a staff member, and we encountered the church secretary along the way. I made an off-the-cuff remark to her about the thickness of the church worship guide, joking that it rivaled the works of John Owen. I didn't realize how cutting my remark sounded. The staff member called me later that afternoon and graciously confronted me about my remark, and I called and apologized to her. It was a throwaway remark, but my thoughtless jesting hurt her feelings. My heart needed to change so that my words were chastened and God-honoring, even in the mundane times.

A couple of years ago a historian friend told me about a conversation he had over dinner with another historian friend. Half-joking, my friend remarked that a recent strain on their friendship had likely been caused by the other's jealousy of his voluminous publishing activities. His comment angered the other man and fractured their friendship for years. Only recently have they reconciled. Maybe the offended party was a little thin-skinned. Perhaps, but mundane words mean a lot.

But it's not only the mundane words. Jesus says all of them matter. Bitter words arise from a bitter heart. Discontented words arise from a discontented heart. Critical words arise from a critical heart. Flattering words arise from a deceptive heart. Defamatory words arise from a heart where the love of Jesus seems to have not taken up residence. Our talk tells us what truly rules our heart. Whatever rules your heart shapes your words. As John Newton (1725–1807) warned his congregation at Olney, sinful talk is where professions of faith die a thousand deaths:

The man who seems, and who desires to be thought, religious may have many qualifications to support his claim, which may be valuable and commendable in themselves, and yet are of no avail to the professor if he bridleth not his tongue. He may have much religious knowledge … He may have a warm zeal, and may contend earnestly for the faith once delivered to the saints. He may be able to talk well on spiritual subjects, to pray with freedom and fervency; yea, he may be a preacher, and acquit himself to the satisfaction of sincere Christians: or he may be a fair trader, a good neighbor, a kind master, an affectionate husband or parent, be free from gross vices, and attend constantly upon the ordinances. Will not such a man seem to himself, and probably be esteemed by others, to be religious? Yet if, with these good properties, he does not bridle his tongue, he may be said to want the one thing needful. He deceiveth his own heart; his religion is vain.[11]

## GRACE BREAKS IN

Sometimes ungodly words arise from an unchanged heart in those who remain outside God's grace. But ungodly words also arise from unmortified sin in the heart of believers. Does this all sound like a lot of bad news? That's why Jesus came—to give us hope and the ability to conquer sin temporally that he conquered eternally at Calvary. But that's chapter four, and before we get to the good news, it's important to come closer to all the ways our restless, sinful hearts manifest themselves in our words.

## MEMORY VERSE

*If anyone thinks he is religious and does not bridle his tongue but deceived his heart, this person's religion is worthless.* (James 1:26)

## QUESTIONS FOR GROUP DISCUSSION

1.  What do the stories of John Rocker, Richard Nixon, and Justine Sacco tell you about the destructive power of words? Can you think of a time

---

11.  John Newton, "Thoughts on the Government of the Tongue" in *The Works of John Newton*, vol. 4 (Edinburgh: Banner of Truth, 2015), 585–86.

when you said some things, perhaps about another person, that had it become public, might have ruined you?

2. How frightened would you be if God could play a tape that would publicly reveal everything you've ever said, even things you've said in private moments? How would that affect even the most intimate relationships with those closest to you?

3. Why does Paul Tripp argue that the book of Proverbs is most fundamentally a treatise on talk? Is it true that you've never spoken a neutral word in your life?

4. How do the many verses in Proverbs show that words are moving either in the direction of life or death?

5. Choose five verses from Proverbs from the many listed in Appendix 2, and discuss them, particularly in light of this question: How would this verse change the way I talk to others?

6. How should Proverbs 18:21 affect how we communicate with others: "Death and life are in the power of the tongue, and those who love it will eat its fruits"?

7. James 3 seems to demonstrate that small things can exercise an oversized effect on our lives. Think of some small conversations that have brought big trouble into your life. Then think of some small conversations that have brought massive joy and even needed change into your life.

8. According to James 3, how is the tongue like a fire? How is it like a rudder? Like a wild animal? What would be the effect if we could remove every single verbal sin from our lives?

9. Given Jesus's words in Matthew 12, how does our talk function as an X-ray machine that reveals the contents of our hearts? What does Jesus mean by "heart"?

10. Is it fair to say that our words will either justify or condemn us on the last day? How does that square with Paul's teaching in Romans and other epistles that says we are justified by faith?

11. Discuss what Jesus means by Matthew 12:36–37. Discuss some of the words you've used over the past week: taken alone from the rest of our life, would they tend to justify or condemn you? How would you like to see change in the way you talk to others?

## FOR FURTHER READING
## AND STUDY

- *Relationships: A Mess Worth Making* (New Growth Press, 2006) by Timothy S. Lane and Paul David Tripp
- "Thoughts on the Government of the Tongue" in *The Works of John Newton*, vol. 4 (Banner of Truth, 2015)

# CHAPTER 3

# WORDS
# AS WEAPONS

*Let no corrupting talk come out of your mouth, but only as is good for building up, as fits the occasion, that it might give grace to those who hear. (Eph. 4:29)*

*Dirty little secrets, dirty little lies; we've got our dirty little fingers in everybody's pies. We love to cut you down to size, we love dirty laundry*
—Eagles singer and songwriter Don Henley, in his 1982 solo hit "Dirty Laundry"

*Sanford and Son* was one of the most popular sitcoms of the 1970s. Foul-mouthed comedian Red Foxx and Pentecostal preacher Demond Wilson co-starred as a junk dealer and his son who lived and ran their business in the Watts neighborhood of Los Angeles. Both the outside and inside of their home/business looked more like the aftermath of a Category 5 hurricane than living space for a family.

Foxx played Fred Sanford, a crusty curmudgeon who ran the business with his son, Lamont, played by Wilson. *Sanford and Son*'s cast of characters were memorable, to say the least. There were Fred's buddies—Grady, Bubba, and Skillet—who frequently stopped by to chat or watch TV with Fred (they always seemed to be watching boxing or monster movies) and usually walked head-long into some kind of absurd drama. There was Lamont's buddy, Rollo, who came off as a little shady, perhaps because Fred always often referred to him as a jailbird. To me, the funniest character was the show's undisputed champion of high drama, Fred's sister-in-law and Lamont's aunt, Esther Anderson. "Aunt Esther" appeared in virtually every episode. Scripted as a devout Christian (and a Baptist), Esther was always armed with her massive, black, KJV Bible, and Fred Sanford was her bitter enemy—stemming from her disapproval of Fred's marriage to her now-deceased sister. She was a clearinghouse for how a Christian should *not* use words.

Esther would come through the front door of the Sanford home/business, and Fred would immediately wrinkle up his face as if he'd smelled sun-simmered road kill. He would immediately lob an insult toward his sister-in-law, usually calling her one of the more popular zoo animals. Never to be outdone, Esther would often as not quote Scripture, usually reminding Fred that he was facing God's eternal judgment for being an "old heathen." The tart-tongued Baptist sister would spar with Fred Sanford, and they would swap insult for insult, blow for blow, with Esther sometimes even swinging her big Bible (and her even larger purse) at her brother-in-law like a George Foreman roundhouse. Often, after hurling a few Scripture verses Fred's way, she'd conclude the bout with the knockout apologetic blow: "Fred Sanford, my Bible says that the wicked will not inherit the kingdom of God, so you'd better make things right with your Maker, you ole fish-eyed fool." Some evangelist, that aunt Esther.

Granted, *Sanford and Son* may seem like an absurd illustration or an anachronistic cultural reference, but I think it illustrates well the disconnect many Christians fail to see between the words that pour forth from their mouths, the allegiance they profess to the Savior, and the true condition of their hearts.

As we saw in chapter two, Jesus believed every syllable that comes out of our mouths is of paramount importance. Solomon, Paul, and James did, too. For further evidence of the heinousness of sinful talk, James 1:26 says: "If anyone thinks he is religious and does not bridle his tongue but deceives his heart, *this person's religion is worthless*" (emphasis mine).

Encapsulated in the typical conversation between the "Christian" Esther and the "pagan" Fred Sanford is a tour de force of the many ways we sin with our tongues. These appear in various lists of sins in Scripture, in places like Ephesians 4:31: "Let all bitterness and wrath and anger and clamor and slander be put away from you, along with all malice" (which sits near 4:29, a key verse in this discussion that will be taken up later).

Scripture speaks of sinful speech in several different categories, and the exchanges in that old 1970s show pretty much hit them all—not good, since one of the dialogue partners was always touted as a follower of Christ, but instructive for us.

Proverbs 18:20-21 helps us place words into one of two categories—words of death and words of life:

> For the fruit of a man's mouth his stomach is satisfied; he is satisfied by the yield of his lips. Death and life are in the power of the tongue, and those who love it will eat its fruits.

Really, for the follower of Christ there are only two types of words: sinful words, which bring death to the hearer (and perhaps even to the hard-hearted speaker) and words of life, which Ephesians 4:29 calls words of grace:

> Let no corrupting talk come out of your mouths, but only as is good for building up, as fits the occasion, that it may give grace to those who hear.

In his classic exposition of *Pilgrim's Progress*, Scottish pastor Alexander Whyte (1836-1921) introduces Bunyan's character "Talkative" by reminding readers that sins of the tongue are such a prevalent theme in Scripture, the topic should receive far more attention from the church than it often does:

> Since we all have a tongue, and since so much of our time is taken up with talk, a simple catalogue of the sins of the tongue is enough to terrify us. The sins of the tongue take up a much larger space in the Bible than we would believe till we have begun to suffer from other men's tongues and especially from our own. The Bible speaks a great deal more and a great deal plainer about the sins of the tongue than any of our pulpits dare to do.[1]

---

1.   Alexander Whyte, *The Characters in Pilgrim's Progress* (Grand Rapids: Baker, 1976), 180.

Yes, the Bible addresses our talk, but in my experience sermons rarely do. I've been in church for five decades and remember only two sermons on the tongue, both from the book of James. With social media and other internet communication, we probably talk more than at any time in history, yet I wonder if we're simply too busy talking to stop and examine *how* we are doing it. After all, we don't want to interrupt ourselves! If online discussion is any indication, the quality of our discourse is at an all-time low. Our talk needs to change.

Perhaps we need first to be terrified by the law before we are able to feel the comfort of the gospel, so let's examine the sinful ways we talk in nine categories.

## 1. GOSSIP AND SLANDER: CATASTROPHIC COUSINS

### GOSSIP

Joseph Stowell calls them "catastrophic cousins," and it wouldn't be difficult to make the case that they destroy more relationships and cause more church splits than any other spiritual disease: slander and gossip.[2] Gossip is slightly different from slander because it's often done in the context of idle, careless chatter, he argues, and I agree.[3]

Oh, how the sons and daughters of Adam love gossip. One cliché says this sin is primarily the domain of women, but I disagree. We men are highly skilled at gossip as well. Think about how your ears perk up when someone begins a conversation with "Hey, did you hear what's been happening with our old friend Jim?" or "Hey, I probably shouldn't tell you this, but you know what Jenny told me about Suzie?" Those words tend to grab our undivided attention.

Gossip appeals to us because sinners love "dirty laundry." We love it when people lose, especially those whom we may (sinfully) view as being a few layers above or below us on the social, economic, educational, or celebrity strata. We love to hear—and spread—bad news about them. Don Henley nailed this truth in his 1982 hit song "Dirty Laundry." The lyrics were

---

2.  Joseph M. Stowell, *The Weight of Your Words: Measuring the Impact of What You Say* (Chicago: Moody, 1998), 22.
3.  Ibid.

intended to critique the perceived yellow journalism of mainstream news media, but what Henley saw as true of reporters can be said of us all:

Dirty little secrets, dirty little lies
We've got our dirty little fingers in everybody's pies
We love to cut you down to size
We love dirty laundry

Gossip is appealing to us because we love stories—about us and others. As Matthew C. Mitchell points out, we read our children stories from the time they were born.[4] Gossip is also telling a story, a story that communicates bad news about another person behind that person's back. Mitchell offers three categories that shine a light to help us see deeper into the shaft of this sin:[5]

*Bad information.* Sharing false information or a rumor about another person. It could be something you know is true, you know is false, or is merely a rumor. Rumors about another person can be devastating because once they've left your mouth and gone into the ears of at least one listener, they are irretrievable. Rumors are like feathers in a pillow—once they've been let out into the wind, it's impossible to get them back in. They spread uncontrollably, and they damage and destroy the reputations of others. With social media, it really doesn't matter whether it's true. What matters is that it supports your cause or viewpoint.

*Bad news about someone.* This is when you share a true story that shames or otherwise paints a person in the worst possible light. I had a friend whose wife caught him looking at pornography. They were working through the matter with our elders, but another man told me and others all about it. He didn't like the other man, so he spread news about his fall far and wide, damaging the other man. We wound up confronting the man who'd gleefully gossiped, and he eventually left the church, while the man who had looked at pornography was restored.

*Bad news for someone.* Scripture depicts gossip as whispering that ruins relationships and separates even the closest of friends: "A dishonest man spreads strife, and a whisperer (gossip) separates close friends" (Prov. 16:28).

---

4.   Matthew C. Mitchell, *Resisting Gossip: Winning the War of the Wagging Tongue* (Fort Washington, PA: CLC Publications, 2013), 25.

5.   Ibid., 24–27.

When you hear gossip about a friend, it plants suspicion in your mind, which builds a barrier of doubt. By the same token, if your friend gossips to you about somebody else, you'll certainly wonder if he gossips about you to others. It destroys trust and creates cynicism within relationships. Gossiping words are killing words.

Even the Preacher in Ecclesiastes makes a whimsical reference to the certainty that all sinful humans, at one time or another, will talk about another person behind their back. He warns against being thin-skinned when you hear that things have been said about you: "Do not take to heart all the things that people say, lest you hear your servant cursing you. Your heart knows that many times you yourself have cursed others" (Eccles. 7:21–22).

## SLANDER

Slander is the open, intentional sharing of damaging information about another person.[6] This is the triple play of sinful talk because it harms the speaker, the hearer, and the one about whom it is spoken.

No matter which English translation you read, slander is mentioned dozens and dozens of times in the Bible. Slander is a species of gossip. It's communicating damaging information about another person with the intention of smearing their character. In journalism it's called "malice aforethought." That is, telling a story—it can be subgenre true or false—with the intent of causing harm to their reputation. In Eden, Satan slandered God when he told our first parents: "You will not surely die. For God knows that when you eat of [the fruit] your eyes will be opened, and you will be like God, knowing good and evil" (Gen. 3:4–5).

Satan slandered God by communicating something about him that wasn't true. The Devil subtly sought to make God out to be a liar (God said they would die, but they won't) and a miserly deity who wants to keep to himself all the power and good things (you could be as great as God, but he won't tell you how to do that).

Slander usually flows out of another sin: envy. The Greek word for *devil* literally means "slanderer." James 4:11–12 points out the seriousness of slander:

---

6. Stowell, *The Weight of Your Words*, 40.

Do not speak evil against one another, brothers. The one who speaks against a brother or judges his brother, speaks evil against the law and judges the law. But if you judge the law, you are not a doer of the law but a judge.

Slander is devilish speech that breaks fellowship among followers of Christ and breaks the royal law (the moral law as summarized in the Ten Commandments). When we speak falsely against a fellow believer, we speak not only against the person, but also against the law of God. In so doing, James argues, the slanderer sets himself illicitly as a judge above the law. Instead of being judged by God's Word, the slanderer judges it.

What's the heart issue behind slander and gossip? The narcissistic duo of self-love and self-promotion. When we traffic in slander and gossip, we tear others down and build ourselves up. Stowell lists several self-centered impulses that drive us to undermine the good name of another person and make ourselves look good:[7]

- Curiosity. We are naturally curious, so we want to know the news. Curiosity is fine, even constructive, unless it leads us down the path toward tearing others down with our information. First Timothy 5:13 links being a busybody with gossips. In that case, curiosity has been left unchecked. Solomon says the slanderer is utterly untrustworthy: "Whoever goes about slandering reveals secrets, but he who is trustworthy in spirit keeps a thing covered" (Prov. 11:13).
- A desire to be the center of attention. We have the scoop on a person of interest to others, juicy information that no one else seems to have.
- The opportunity to elevate ourselves. As Will Durant said, "To speak ill of others is a dishonest way of praising ourselves."[8]
- Malicious words are often spawned by bitterness. I once had a colleague in journalism who spread the worst information about his boss, because the slanderer had applied for the job for which our boss had been hired. My colleague vented often as a seeming act of revenge against our boss. He was utterly unaware of how bad it made him look.

7. Ibid.
8. Ibid., 41.

When I was young, someone started a rumor that one of the prominent women in my home church was having an adulterous affair with a wealthy business owner in town. It was false, pure slander, but her husband believed it and eventually took his own life over it. This is why Paul commanded the church at Ephesus, "Let all bitterness and wrath and anger and clamor and slander be put away from you, along with all malice" (Eph. 4:31). Slander and gossip kill churches, ruin marriages, destroy friendships—and worse.

## 2. CRITICAL TALK: YOU'RE NO GOOD

I won't spend a lot of space on criticism, because I think it's a sub-genre of slander and gossip. Critics are everywhere—the workplace, the ballpark, the car, the mall, and, especially, the church.

My father, a developer and master builder of custom homes, used to say, "Everybody thinks they're a builder." By that, he meant many of his customers thought they knew how to build a better house than he did. Virtually anyone who works with the public—policemen, teachers or church leaders—knows all too well what it means to be criticized. Christians are by no means exempt from sinful criticism.

Gracious, instructive critique is often valid and helpful. It should not be confused with the type of sinful criticism I have in mind here. Jesus had his critics—the Pharisees, Sadducees and various other religious leaders. Moses had severe critics among the Israelites. Paul had his critics among friends and foes alike. Throughout human history, God has endured many critics. Guards at the Communist concentration camps after World War II often scoffed blasphemously at Christian prisoners while they were beating them, "Where is your God now? Is he not powerful enough to rescue you from prison?"[9] God's critics are myriad and will abound until Jesus returns.

Why do we criticize? Because we think more highly of ourselves than we ought. We criticize our pastor's sermons because, in our heart of hearts, we're certain we could be more engaging, preach shorter sermons, say things better, and interpret the Bible better. We criticize our spouses or kids because they don't meet our unreasonable expectations. We criticize our boss because he dares hold us accountable for the quantity and quality of work

---

9.  The Voice of the Martyrs, *Wurmbrand: Tortured for Christ—The Complete Story* (Colorado Springs: David C. Cook, 2018), 228.

we were hired to do. We criticize our church because it fails to meet our standards of music or education or leadership or vision. We criticize because we are self-centered, not others-centered, not God-centered. Far too often, our criticism is a failure to love God and to love our neighbor as ourselves (Mark 12:30–31).

Why do I say that?

Because in our drive to criticize, we say things about people we'd never consider saying about God. Sure, there are times when we do things that deserve critique. But when we criticize others wrongly, we are speaking ill of his image-bearers, which is to say we are really criticizing God. James 3:9–10 makes this point clear:

> With [the tongue], we bless our Lord and Father, and with it we curse people who are made in the likeness of God. From the same mouth come blessing and cursing. My brothers, these things ought not to be so.

Jealousy also often drives criticism. We envy what another person has or who they are in terms of societal stature or profession. We can't be them, so we denigrate them, cut them down to size. The Pharisees are a prime example. They hated Jesus in part because they envied him. Many had left their fold and begun to follow him. Jealousy, in part, led them to crucify our Lord. Ungodly criticism is a subtle-but-ugly sin that's common to us all.

### 3. SARCASM: BUILD ME UP, TEAR YOU DOWN

There are two kinds of sarcasm. First, there is what we might call good-natured teasing. It's light-hearted, even intimate, and can bring much-needed humor to a tense situation—think here of well-done satire. Real life can be awfully funny. But there's another type of sarcasm that's sinful—and by no means humorous. We traffic in this kind of sarcasm when we get off a "zinger" and make others laugh when we've "scored a point" against another person by making them feel small. Such sarcasm draws attention to me, amounts to a failure to love my neighbor as myself, and exposes me as a fool: "Whoever belittles his neighbor lacks sense, but a man of understanding remains silent" (Prov. 11:12). When I'm tempted to "get one off" on another person, it's better to keep my mouth shut and demonstrate wisdom.

Sinful sarcasm is akin to the mocking and scorning Jesus endured while suffering on the cross.[10] "He saved others, why can't he save himself? He is the King of Israel; let him come down now from the cross, and we will believe in him. He trusts in God; let God deliver him now, if he desires him. For he said, 'I am the Son of God'" (Matt. 27:42–43). The spectators at Calvary that first Good Friday made light of Jesus, scoffing at his claims to be the Son of God, making themselves feel powerful while taking advantage of his weakness.

This is what sinful sarcasm does.

It makes me look clever by making you look foolish. We can do this subtly as Christians, as parents, as church leaders. Pastors can use sinful sarcasm in the pulpit. I once heard a well-known leader in my denomination use his wife as an illustration of a country hick. He set it up by touting his degrees from an Ivy League school, then made fun of the way she pronounced his name and how growing up in a rural area had left her intellectually slow. He referenced the creepy 1970s movie *Deliverance*. It was probably unintentional—and I'll assume his motives were pure—but he built himself up by tearing her down. Many who heard him agreed. I'm glad she wasn't in the audience that day.

Sinful sarcasm violates Paul's instruction in Ephesians 4:29: "Let no corrupting talk come out of your mouth, but only such as is good for building up, as fits the occasion, that it may give grace to those who hear." We should ask: Does my sarcasm build the other person up? If the answer is no, then we shouldn't speak it. Does it give grace to all those who hear (including the audience before whom it is uttered)? Probably not. If it fails this test, then it likely tears the other person down and builds me up. It may also discourage those who hear.

Sarcasm also often fails the test of the Golden Rule in which Christ admonishes us to treat others the way we want to be treated. Ask: Do I want to be the butt of another person's joke? Few of us want that. This question

---

10. In 1 Kings 18 Elijah uses sarcasm effectively in his contest with the prophets of Baal. In mocking their false gods, Elijah said, "And at noon Elijah mocked them, saying, 'Cry aloud, for he is a god. Either he is musing, or he is relieving himself, or he is on a journey, or perhaps he is asleep and must be awakened" (1 Kings 18:27). It is appropriate to mock and use sarcasm in the face of false gods. Idolatry demonstrates the foolishness of sinful men and several psalms, including Psalm 2, portray God as laughing at those who reject him. In similar vein, the reformer Martin Luther said he would often scorn and mock the Devil when he felt tempted to think false things about the gospel.

alone, if asked mentally before we spoke, would probably scuttle much of our sinful sarcasm. We want our words to give off the oxygen of God's grace, of edifying and building up others. We must do that without flattering them.

## 4. BOASTING AND FLATTERY: BUILD ME UP, BUILD YOU UP

### BOASTING

One of the Bible verses my dad most often quoted to me and my brothers was Proverbs 27:2:

> Let another praise you, and not your own mouth; a stranger and not your own lips.

He usually related it to our athletic endeavors or to our classroom performance at school. Dad had a sister who seemed to boast virtually every time she opened her mouth, and he didn't want us to be like her because that kind of talk was the opposite of humility.

Christians in general, pastors in particular, would do well to write Proverbs 27:2 over the door of their hearts. What is boasting? It is talking in a proud and self-satisfied way about our achievements, possessions, or abilities. Simply put, boasting is self-idolatry.

Does God hate boasting? Look at what happened to King Nebuchadnezzar in Daniel 3–4. In the ultimate act of hubris and crass idolatry, the king ordered his people to build a golden statue of himself that was around 90 feet tall and commanded the citizens of Babylon to worship it. As God made resoundingly clear in Isaiah 42:8, "I am the LORD, that is my name; my glory I give to no other, nor my praise to carved idols." As punishment for his self-idolatry, God caused Nebuchadnezzar to lose his mind and to lose his kingdom. The Lord sent him to live in a pasture with the beasts of the field, "until you know that the Most High rules the kingdom of men and gives it to whom he will." As punishment for his idolatry, Nebuchadnezzar became subhuman. Never, ever take glory that belongs to God alone. Don't boast. Seek humility. Glory thieves will be punished severely. Taking glory that was never meant for humans makes us subhuman.

Another frightening account that reads like the script for a Boris Karloff film is the story of Herod in Acts 12:21–23. After Herod delivered an oration to the people, his audience began to chant, "The voice of a god, and not of a man!" In his pride, Herod accepted praise that belongs to God alone. Look what happens next: "Immediately an angel of the Lord struck him down, because he did not give God the glory, and he was eaten by worms and breathed his last" (Acts 12:23). Boasting is a first cousin to pride, and God will share his glory with no man.

But boasting is usually much more subtle than accepting direct worship. None of us will likely ever face that temptation. Boasting can be done under the guise of a prayer request: "Before my children are allowed to open gifts at Christmas, we go from fire station to fire station giving bread they've spent days baking to the firemen who have to work on that day, and then we go to the homeless shelter to work. Only then do we go home and open gifts. Pray that we'll have good gospel conversations." That was an actual prayer request in a church I have led. Or, "My son made the dean's list at college—just like I did every semester when I was in college. Pray he will stay humble." Right on.

Boasting can be done in the pulpit. I heard a (non-prosperity gospel) pastor say this during a sermon: "We own three homes—a beach house, a mountain house, and of course the 4,000-square-foot house we live in. Our mountain house was nearly hit by last week's tornado." I'm not sure the pastor intended to boast, but that was how I heard it.

Boasting can also amount to virtue signaling. During college, a Christian girl I knew presented a paper in class called "Why I'm Still a Virgin" in which she basically said she didn't want to be trashy like the other girls on campus. Not many of us would do that, but we might post selfies showing the Instagram world we did our quiet time this morning. Box checked. Jesus might not be as impressed as our friends: "Beware of practicing your righteousness before other people in order to be seen by them, for then you will have no reward from your Father who is in heaven" (Matt. 6:1).

Boasting is a failure to count others as better than ourselves, contrary to Paul's admonition in Philippians 2:3, "Do nothing from selfish ambition or conceit, but in humility count others more significant than yourselves." Conceit is the worst form of competition, in pride lifting ourselves up and inflating ourselves above others.

It's hard to imagine a greater experience than being called to meet with God in glory and then be sent back to earth. This is precisely what happened to Paul in 2 Corinthians 12, but the apostle wouldn't even talk about it. He didn't want to be tempted to brag. Scripture calls us to only one kind of boasting: in Jesus Christ, in his person and work. Boasting in anything but

Christ is antithetical to the gospel and antithetical to the way God works: "God chose what is low and despised in the world, even things that are not, to bring to nothing things that are, so that no human being might boast in the presence of God ... 'Let the one who boasts, boast in the Lord'" (1 Cor. 1:28–29, 31b). Paul didn't boast in his experience, but in his weakness, which is instructive for us.

To be a braggart is to be a glory thief—pilfering what belongs to God alone. Boast in Christ and in his finished work at Calvary.

## FLATTERY

In college, one of my friends sometimes wore a t-shirt with the words "flattery will get you everywhere" emblazoned across the front. But we all know that flattery is a false friend. When I flatter another person, I place them in my debt by verbally commending some action, virtue, or involvement in their life.[11] Flattery is self-centered. Why? Because when I flatter you, you pay attention to me. I tell you that you might be one of the best teachers I've ever heard. You'll probably stop and listen. Sometimes, we are so starved for attention, we use undue adulation to get it.[12] Or, we flatter others so they will return the compliment. Or, we flatter to gain the other person's respect rather than by being patient and earning it through building a loyal, long-term relationship.

There are dozens of verses in the Bible that forbid flattery, that decry flattering lips. King David speaks of boasting and flattery to illustrate the abysmal, godless, proud state of our fallen world in Psalm 12:2–4. Don't miss the number of ways he speaks of sins that arise from the tongue, especially when we use words as a weapon:

> Everyone utters lies to his neighbor;
> with flattering lips and a double heart they speak.
> May the LORD cut off all flattering lips,
> the tongue that makes great boasts,
> those who say, "With our tongue we shall prevail,
> our lips are with us; who is master over us?"

---

11. Stowell, *Weight of Your Words*, 52.
12. Ibid.

In the end, flattery is a subtle form of lying. You say something nice about someone to put them under your power. You don't really mean it. The psalmist speaks to the double-tongued nature of a false friend who butters up a person out of dubious heart motives—the flattery was a form of betrayal: "His speech was smooth as butter, yet war was in his heart; his words were softer than oil, yet they were drawn swords" (Ps. 55:31). Sadly, many of us enjoy the flattery! Instead, perhaps we should pray for the flatterer, for really, he is spreading a trap for us: "A man who flatters his neighbor spreads a net for his feet" (Prov. 29:5).

Instead of flattery, we should offer encouraging compliments to others that give ultimate glory to God. We could say, "The Lord has blessed you with a beautiful family" or "I am grateful the Lord has given me such an honest and caring friend as you" or "The Lord has blessed you with physical beauty/a brilliant mind." Different from flattery, the encouraging compliment grounds the kind words in the goodness of God and doesn't give the appearance that I really just want to put you in my debt. It's what the writer of Proverbs has in mind when he wrote, "A word fitly spoken is like apples of gold in a setting of silver" (Prov. 25:11).

Here's the bottom line with boasting and flattery: more often than not, both of them arise from insecurity and a failure to find our ultimate identity in Christ. We want to be known for how skilled we are at our vocations (we're hard-working), how many books we read in a year (we're smart), how attractive is our appearance (we're beautiful), or myriad other things, so we boast. We want you to think highly of us, so we flatter. It's better to avoid both and find our sufficiency and identity in Christ and in who he is making us and in what he is doing in us.

## 5. LIES AND DECEIT

Truth-telling isn't popular these days. Our culture has shifted to an ethic of expediency and self-promotion, such that falsehood is tolerated, even encouraged. I mean, is anybody's life really as good as their Facebook or Instagram profile would have you think? All my high school friends seem so healthy, wealthy, and wise. But that's just a "small lie," right? As Mark Twain once quipped, "When in doubt, tell the truth. It will confound your enemies and astound your friends."[13] Of course, truth has always been Satan's favor-

---

13. Ibid., 23.

ite target—Scripture calls him the father of lies (John 8:44). Lying is Satan's native tongue, so it stands to reason he will attack truth everywhere he sees it. We get a hint of this satanic sentiment in Jesus's sham trial en route to Calvary, when Pilate responded to Jesus's declaration that he came into the world to bear witness to the truth by cynically asking, "What is truth?" Truth does not matter to skeptics who have despaired of knowing it. Such is the milieu we inhabit in the 21st century.

In his powerful prayer of repentance in Psalm 51, David says this in verse 6: "Behold, you delight in truth in the inward being, and you teach me wisdom in the secret heart." Truth and wisdom are at the center of our being, and truth stands at the heart of the Christian faith. In his well-known words in John 14:6, Jesus describes himself as "the way, the truth, and the life." Jesus is "full of grace and truth" (John 1:14). John describes the Holy Spirit as "the Spirit of truth," whose primary mission is to guide God's people into an apprehension of all truth (John 14:17; 16:13).

Truth is absolutely vital for orthodox doctrine and orthodox living, so it almost goes without saying that Christians are a people created by the truth of God's grace so they must be a people committed to telling the truth at all times, which means we must refrain from lying, as the psalmist repeatedly reminds us: "Keep your tongue from evil and your lips from speaking deceit. Turn away from evil and do good; seek peace and pursue it" (Ps. 34:13–14).

How serious a sin is lying? In Acts 5, God killed Ananias and Sapphira for lying to the Holy Spirit about the net worth of a piece of property and a donation of the proceeds of its sale to the Lord's work: "But Peter said, 'Ananias, why has Satan filled your heart to lie to the Holy Spirit and to keep back for yourself part of the proceeds of the land?'" (Acts 5:3). God includes a lying tongue in the list of things God hates in Proverbs 6:17, and liars are included in those whom God will hurl into the lake of fire at the end of time (Rev. 21:8).

In this category of lying, I have in mind deceptive speech of all kinds, including beguiling words and giving a false witness in violation of the ninth commandment. Of course, most (and I hope all) Christians would agree that outright lying is a sin and should be avoided at all times. But what about the "little lies" Fleetwood Mac sings about in their 1987 hit song of the same title? "Tell me lies, tell me sweet little lies." Closer to the truth is the words of country singer Clay Walker's song "Then What?" about a man of deception who gets caught: "You're not anybody anybody's gonna trust." Scripture tells us that the engine of truth brings with it other valuable Christian virtues such as integrity, stability, security, and faith, all of which fall away when truth is compromised. "Little lies" may not come with severe temporal consequences, but they compromise the truth as much as big lies do. For example, some of us grew up watching *The Andy Griffith Show* and see it as wholesome entertainment, good for Christians. And it is—for the most part. But think of all the times the main characters either lied or advocated lying. Many times, Sheriff Andy Taylor would receive a phone call only to have Aunt Bea or Deputy Fife tell them he was not present. Is that an innocent "white lie" since it's on a program fit for family consumption?

Think about how relationships are destroyed by lying. A wife catches her husband lying about where he had been those nights he was alleged to have been working late. Even if he was just bowling with the guys, it's going to take a long time to rebuild trust. Or if a pastor downloads and preaches another man's sermons off the internet and then lies to his congregation by preaching them as if they are his own. Trust won't return soon. Or when your teenager lies about her whereabouts on a Saturday night, and you learn she was drinking beer with friends instead of babysitting. That's going to change things for a good while.

Joseph Stowell points out three reasons why truth is so important to God and should be of utmost importance to his people:[14]

1.  Truth-telling aligns us with God and his Word.
2.  We are redeemed to reflect God's character. Truth is at the heart of the holy character of God. As God's people, we communicate something false about God when we lie.
3.  Truth-telling is a matter of submission to God's will. Proverbs 13:5 says, "A righteous man hates falsehood," and Paul commands believers, "Do not lie to on another, seeing that you have put off the old self with its practices" (Col. 3:9).

14. Ibid., 24.

## 6. ANGRY WORDS AND GRUMBLING WORDS: VOLCANO OR SLOW BOIL

### ANGRY WORDS

We've all heard it, and most of us mouthed it obnoxiously as children: "Sticks and stones will break my bones, but words will never hurt me." If only it were true. Words do hurt, especially when they're being thrown at us in a fit of anger. All of us are prone to anger. We tend to sin with our tongues most when we are angry. Consider Aunt Esther and Fred Sanford as exhibit A. When Fred provoked his sister-in-law, she responded with angry words, sometimes to the extreme.[15] But we do the same, and the first part of Proverbs 12:18 tells us they shouldn't be taken lightly: "There is one whose rash words are like sword thrusts, but the tongue of the wise brings healing." Words of death vs. words of life. Rash words kill. But the writer of Proverbs goes further, calling the angry person a reckless fool (14:16a).

Typically, when we get angry, we talk. When I played baseball as a young man, an umpire's bad call would make me angry. My anger would manifest in words. I had a friend who would do the same when we played golf—an ostensibly genteel sport. He would hit his ball in the rough or the sand trap or (often) the water. He'd call himself names like "idiot" or "moron." One day we were playing in a foursome with two other friends. Every time he hit a bad shot, he spewed colorful syllables, and we'd snicker and tease him. Hole after hole, his frustration grew like water swelling a kinked garden hose. At last, the dam holding back his anger burst: he swung and missed his ball on the 17th tee and followed it with some choice words not fit for print. The three of us playing with him guffawed. We weren't quite expecting what happened next: he unhitched his golf bag from the cart and hurled it (it held his expensive set of Calloway clubs and a Rolex watch, which he'd put in the pocket for safekeeping but had obviously forgotten about it) into the nearby lake. After watching his clubs sink beneath the surface, he sprinted toward the pond and dove in, the water virtually boiling with his heated words.

---

15. Here are a couple of resources I've found helpful for helping deal with the heart of anger, both personally and pastorally: Robert D. Jones, *Uprooting Anger: Biblical Help for a Common Problem* (Phillipsburg, NJ: P&R, 2005) and Edward T. Welch, *A Small Book about a Big Problem: Meditations on Anger, Patience, and Peace* (Greensboro, NC: New Growth Press, 2018).

Three decades later, we still laugh about that incident—and so does my formerly angry friend, now a follower of Christ. But Scripture doesn't consider his anger and the resulting words a laughing matter: "A fool gives full vent to his anger, but a wise man quietly holds it back (Prov. 29:11).

Anger brings forth words that cause problems far more serious than an interrupted recreational golf game. A husband insults his wife during an argument: "You're stupid" or "You're ugly" or "You're a terrible person." The result is a damaged relationship and perhaps a psychologically damaged wife. A teenage son unloads on his father in anger: "I hate you and everything you stand for." Ouch. That's going to take some repentance and work to heal. Or an angry church member explodes at his pastor: "I wish we'd never called you to be our pastor. I voted against you, and wish I could do it all over again. You're an idiot." Major damage to the pastor and his relationship to the member follow in the wake of those ill-advised words.

Our anger is profoundly different from God's. His anger is always righteous, always directed at things like sin, evil, and injustice. He hates evil (Prov. 8:13), dishonest scales (Prov. 20:10), haughty eyes, a lying tongue, murderers, schemers, false witnesses, and those who stir up dissension among God's people (Prov. 6:16–19). We get angry over golf, our failure to diet, our husband's domineering of the radio, and a thousand other petty things. We weaponize our words to repay those whom we think have wronged us in some way—personal slights, attacks, or favoritism. Sinful words spoken in anger are ungodly—they are the opposite of God's character.

When God is wronged by us, like a loving father, he still has our best interests in mind, and this is evident in how he responds. Consider the golden calf incident in Exodus 32. God's people are at Sinai, and they anger him by fashioning and worshiping an idol. In Exodus 33, God responds by commanding them to leave Sinai, but he doesn't fly off the handle as we do at the least perceived slight. No, in Exodus 33:1–3, God reiterates his promise to take them to the promised land—even though they have just rejected him for other gods. He puts his anger on simmer and does not destroy them—their sin (and ours) deserves utter destruction. And in 33:12–22, he gives the people grace through Moses's intercession for them—a clear picture of Christ as intercessor. Still, the people's murmuring against God came with severe consequences: that generation did not enter the promised land.

But, mercifully, God's anger qualitatively differs from ours, and his anger should shape ours. Ephesians 4:26–27 seems to indicate that there is a righteous anger and an unrighteous anger: "Be angry and do not sin; do not

let the sun go down on your anger, and give no opportunity to the devil."
Not all anger is sin—Jesus ejecting the moneychangers from the temple is
one example—but the believer should not be consumed by anger. Ungodly anger gives opportunity to the Devil—and he most often rides in on an
unbridled tongue.

Paul compiled several lists of sins (Rom. 1:21–32; 1 Cor. 6:9–10; Gal. 5:19–
21; Col. 3:5–9; Titus 3:3). Look at the one in Galatians 5:19–21: It shows that
human beings are bent toward sexual immorality and anger. And we should
have at least as much concern about anger and its divisive, destructive ways
as we do about sexual immorality.[16] The ways anger is expressed usually pour
forth from our mouths: enmity, strife, jealousy, fits of anger (my buddy's bad
day at the golf course), rivalries, dissensions, divisions, wrath, malice, and
slander. Reckless anger devastates our families and relationships, and tears
apart our churches.

When we think of anger, we tend to envision an angry person exploding like a volcano, but that's not the only way sinful human express anger.
Some people's anger is more of a simmer, and it's often expressed in grumbling—another universal (and sometimes subtle) sin that arises in our talk.

## GRUMBLING

Brother John entered the "Monastery of Silence," and the abbot informed
him he was welcome to serve as a monk there, but reminded him it was
a silent monastery. "You may only speak when I give you permission," he
told John. After five years, Brother John was allowed to speak two words. He
chose, "Hard bed." "I'm sorry to hear that, we'll get you a new one," the abbot
said. Another five years passed before he was given permission to speak two
more words: "Cold food." John received assurance the food would improve.
On his 15th anniversary of entering the monastery, the abbot again granted
him two more words: "I quit," John said. To this, the abbot replied, "It's probably best; you've done nothing but complain since you got here."[17]

This humorous, fictional story well illustrates how we really are: In our
fallenness, our hearts are naturally bent toward expressing discontentment
through grousing and complaining. To demonstrate this, usually all I have to

16. Edward T. Welch, *A Small Book about a Big Problem: Meditations on Anger, Patience, and Peace*
(Greensboro, NC: New Growth Press, 2018), 88.
17. William B. Barcley, *The Secret of Contentment* (Phillipsburg, NJ: P&R, 2010), 49.

do is assign—out of the blue—a chore to my teenage children. I don't think it would be terribly inaccurate if I were to speculate that my children's least favorite Bible verse is Philippians 2:14: "Do all things without grumbling or disputing."

They probably have an aversion to that verse because my wife and I have used it so often—perhaps misused it at times—as a catalyst to get them to do some chore around the house. But there's a lot more to Paul's seven-word command than meets the eye and more importance to it than merely employing it as a verse to clobber adolescent laziness. Why is it so important? It seems a little petty, maybe a low-level sin. (After all, weren't we merely offering a prayer request when we told our friends to ask God to give me one job instead of three?)

It's important because it's subtle—like those germs we don't see on the shopping cart that wind up giving us the flu. It's important because God hates grumbling. This we know from God's response to the incessant complaining of his old covenant people. Paul tells the church at Philippi to refrain from grumbling because of how the Israelites groaned about the bitter water and having a menu consisting only of the bread from heaven God provided them in the wilderness. They grumbled about Moses's leadership—a reality to which most every pastor can relate. In what is almost a humorous understatement, Numbers 21:4b says, "And the people became impatient on the way" to the promised land. They groused and moaned immediately after leaving Egypt, complained all along the way, and finally grumbled just before they made it to the Holy Land.

After the Israelites complained about the bread ("We loathe this worthless food," Num. 21:5), upset that they had no meat, even wondering if life as slaves in Egypt was superior to their present circumstances in the wilderness with God. Moses told them: "Your grumbling is not against us but against God" (Ex. 16:8; cf. 15:24; 26:7–9; Num. 20–21). Their grumbling was a crime against God, one so serious that the Lord sent fiery serpents to bite them (Num. 21:6) and sentenced them to 40 years of wandering in the wilderness. Paul calls the Old Testament accounts of their grumpiness toward God an example, written for our instruction (1 Cor. 10:11). Just prior to that, he said grumbling is "putting Christ to the test." Therein lies the seriousness of this kind of sinful talk.

Grumbling or complaining is a capital offense for the very reason Paul gave: it puts God to the test. It says we could do a better job of writing our life story. Grumbling is discontentment expressed verbally. And it reveals the condition of our hearts because to grumble is to say, "I don't like my circumstances, I don't think they're fair, and if I could write the script for my life, it would be far better and would make me far happier." Complaining subtly questions the wisdom and sovereignty of God.

In his not-so-subtly titled sermon *The Hellish Sin of Discontent*, Scottish Presbyterian pastor Thomas Boston (1676–1732) said discontentment that leads to grumbling and complaining is the same as the sin of covetousness—you desire to an idolatrous degree something God hasn't been pleased to give you, whether it's a different city to live in, a more agreeable husband, smarter children, a better church, or a fatter bank account. Discontentment puts God in the dock. Boston gives several reasons why discontentment is such a grave sin, tantamount to spiritual adultery:[18]

- Discontentment mistrusts God. It holds him in contempt.
- Discontentment amounts to complaining against God's plan.
- Discontentment reflects a desire to be sovereign.
- Discontentment covets something God has not been pleased to give us.
- Discontentment subtly (or not so subtly) communicates that God has made a mistake.
- Discontentment denies the wisdom of God and exalts my wisdom. This was at the heart of the first sin in Eden: "Has God really said?"

The verse that follows Philippians 2:14 tells us what happens when we stop complaining: we shine with the reflected beauty of Jesus.

> Do all things without grumbling or disputing, that you may be blameless and innocent, children of God without blemish in the midst of a crooked and twisted generation, among whom you shine as lights in the world. (Phil. 2:14–15)

## JUDGMENTAL WORDS

In the 1970s and '80s, America's favorite Bible verse was John 3:16, but my friend Harry Reeder argues—and I think he's correct—that at the end of the

---

18. Thomas Boston, "The Hellish Sin of Discontent" in *The Complete Works of Thomas Boston*, vol. 2 (London: Tentmaker Publications, ND), 505.

second decade of the 2000s, it's now Matthew 7:1: "Judge not, that you be not judged."

Judgmental speech may be widely condemned today, but it's always been in vogue among the sons of Adam. Job's three friends are perhaps Scripture's illustration in Scripture par excellence. They came to their suffering friend, ostensibly to comfort him in the wake of his personal tsunami. He had lost all his worldly possessions, all his children, even his health. His friends arrive and chastise Job—God is punishing him for some terrible sin. Granted, they did sit for seven days in silence with Job, mourning his loss. But the trouble started when they opened their mouths. Job is a liar, an unrepentant wretch, a miserable, deceived man whose secret sins are so many, God had little choice but to pour out his temporal wrath on him. Job is a complainer, a crybaby, a cupcake whose motives are of the worst order.

Zophar, Bildad, and Eliphaz judged Job. Jesus's words in Matthew 7:1–5, one of our Lord's most colorful admonitions. Addressing the ever-judgmental Pharisees, Jesus tells them not to judge, because they will be weighed on the same scales by which they measure others. Then he uses an unforgettable—and hilarious—word picture to show why it's so foolish to think we can assess the hearts of others with 20/20 accuracy:

> Why do you see the speck that is in your brother's eye, but do not take the speck out of your eye? Or how can you say to your brother, "Let me take the speck out of your eye," when there is the log in your own eye? You hypocrite, first take the log out of your own eye, and then you will see clearly to take the speck out of your brother's eye. (Matt. 7:3–5)

We use judgmental speech when we use words of certainty to describe uncertain things. Judgmental words most often flow forth as an expression of anger, so they could be categorized as a form of anger. But judgmental words can be subtle, too. They can be something as simple as "I know exactly why you didn't invite me to the party—you don't like me and don't want me around." The problem is, you don't really know why they didn't invite you. Or, you tell your teenage daughter, "I know you're lying to me about this, because you're nothing but a liar" when you don't have evidence that proves that she's lying.

It would be better to graciously ask, "Why didn't you invite me to the party? Have I done something to wrong you or upset you?" Or in the case of the alleged teen liar, "I feel certain you wouldn't lie to me, so you are telling the truth about this, correct?" In both cases, it will keep you from falsely judging the other person and may keep the conversation on a more civil level.

We have the same problem as Job's friends: We aren't omniscient and cannot divine the thoughts and intentions of others' hearts, yet we crave omniscience, which is why we're so prone to judging others.

## 8. CURSING AND TAKING GOD'S NAME IN VAIN

I worked as a newspaper journalist during my younger adult years, and at the outset of my career, I may have possessed the foulest mouth on the entire staff. Sadly, during those years, I was wandering far from the fold of God. In my experience, journalists seem to pride themselves in the ways they use foul language. A former colleague described one of our more colorful editors as the "Paganini[19] of the F-word." Not exactly a compliment in most places, but esteemed in that venue. In the years I played baseball I was ejected from games three times for heaping a hail of four-letter words upon umpires. I grew up around baseball and rationalized it by telling myself that all baseball people cussed—it was as much a part of the game as curve balls and stolen bases. All the while, I claimed to be a Christian.

Decades later, I'm deeply embarrassed by my unsanctified tongue. No doubt, I grieved the Spirit of God and brought shame on the cause of Christ by talking that way while professing to be a Christian. Thankfully, Christ has changed my heart and has placed new words in my mouth.

Still, my experience raises the question: Should Christians use foul language?

The early 2000s witnessed some interesting conversations among Reformed Christians about the use of foul language. I once heard of a pastor whom some called "the cussing preacher"! I have heard debates over this topic with some actually setting forth a case for the strategic use of four-letter words, typically characterizing the apostle Paul as a cursing preacher.[20]

---

19. Niccolo Paganini (1782–1840) was an Italian virtuoso on violin and guitar. Paganini left his mark as the father of modern violin technique and was a skilled composer.

20. I cannot find a published case in support of a Christian using foul language, but have been involved in several private conversations with believers who argue in the affirmative. The most popular argument I've heard to substantiate the Christian's freedom to

But if we are interested at all in obeying Scripture, there really should be no debate. Consider again Paul's words in Ephesians 4:29: "Let no corrupting talk come out of your mouths, but only such as is good for building up, as fits the occasion, that it may give grace to those who hear."

The Greek word the ESV renders "unwholesome" in 4:29 is *sapros*, which literally means "corrupt." That verse by itself seems to answer the question of whether or not a believer should use foul language, but look at what Paul says next in verse 30: "And do not grieve the Holy Spirit of God, by whom you were sealed for the day of redemption."

The inference Paul seems to be making is pretty clear: the destructive use of speech grieves the third person of the Godhead who indwells Christians. In verse 31, Paul follows by alluding to divisive words that quench the Spirit: "Let all bitterness and wrath and anger and clamor and slander be put away from you, along with all malice." Ungodly talk, cursing, as well as slander and gossip, quench the Holy Spirit within us and interrupt our fellowship with a holy God.

Therefore, Christians would be wise to refrain from such language, especially if it involves the name of God. The third commandment makes it clear that God's name is not to be trifled with: "You shall not take the name of the LORD your God in vain, for the Lord will not hold him guiltless who takes his name in vain" (Ex. 20:7). Swearing by God's name or damning others (or inanimate objects) is akin to blasphemy, Puritan Thomas Watson warns: "Swearers, like mad dogs, fly in the face of heaven; and when they are angered, spew out their blasphemous venom on God's sacred majesty."[21]

Paul also offers what seems to be a direct prohibition of swearing in Ephesians 5:4: "Let there be no filthiness nor foolish talk nor crude joking, which are out of place, but instead let there be thanksgiving."

This verse follows Ephesians 5:3, where the apostle forbids talk about sexual immorality, putting it alongside impurity and covetousness as things that "must not even be named among you, as is proper among saints." Some commentators think Paul may have in mind crude talk about sexual immo-

---

use foul language is that Paul did so in Philippians 3:7 where Paul, in the Greek, says he counts everything as "dung" compared to knowing Jesus Christ. Though Paul's term there is a strong word used to emphasize the superiority of Jesus compared to Paul's credentials, I remain unconvinced that it may be marshaled as evidence that we are free to spout four-letter words.

21. Thomas Watson, *The Ten Commandments* (Carlisle, PA: Banner of Truth, 2000), 88.

rality. In verse 4, he encourages believers to replace any crude, offensive talk with words of thanksgiving. What kind of talk is not fitting for a follower of Christ? Filthiness or foolish talk. Instead, what kind of words are most appropriate? Thanksgiving for the grace and mercy we've received in Christ.

In light of Jesus's words in Matthew 12 that we examined in the last chapter—"out of the overflow of the heart, the mouth speaks"—it is important for us to ask, "What is it in my heart that is overflowing in profanity?" Why would I want to use such words when milder, more wholesome words are available to describe the same thing? Frequent use of such language ought to be the occasion for examining our hearts and asking God to show what sins are bubbling up and out of our mouths and resulting in coarse talk. Vulgar talk sullies a Christian's witness before a watching world, but thankfulness makes our faith winsome and compelling. Sure, there are times when we need to speak in a plain, pointed manner; but there are better words available for such occasions than profanity.

It's not only unwholesome talk that makes light of God, Erik Raymond points out. F-bombs and taking God's name in vain aren't the only words that displease, even misrepresent God. Words like "luck" and "fate," when used by Christians, draw a false picture of God and his absolute sovereignty. Luck and fate "are four-letter words that Christians should mortify with quickness. These words and their concepts are unbiblical and atheistic. Luck communicates randomness while fate describes the inevitability of something happening without a purpose. Both are blind and impersonal ... They are Christian cuss words because they undermine the key biblical doctrine of God's providence."[22] Indeed, we must be careful how we talk about God and his work in us and in his world.

## 9. CARELESS WORDS

It's a cliché, but we have to admit there's a lot of truth in it: "Loose lips sink ships." I've heard that many times in my life, but the writer of Proverbs puts it more soberly for the believer: "When words are many, sin is not lacking" (Prov. 10:19a). Still, we talk and talk. And those of us who are big talkers are

22. Erik Raymond, "Christians Need to Stop Cussing," The Gospel Coalition, https://www. thegospelcoalition.org/blogs/erik-raymond/christian-need-to-stop-cussing, accessed June 20, 2019.

in grave danger if we don't learn to curtail our tongues or, at minimum, learn to choose our words carefully and wisely.

We all know a few people (among perhaps we are one of them) whom David Powlison describes as "incessant talkers."[23] If the average talker utters 20,000 words per day, the incessant talker's verbal allotment is two or three times that much. It's fine to be an incessant talker if the talking is coupled with wisdom, but I've met prodigious Christian talkers I would characterize as careless talkers. They don't have a filter on their tongues, and they don't give much, thought to what they say.

I think here of a woman in a church I led whose life verse seemed to be, "I just tell it like it is." When confronted about some loose, sinful words she had used about two elders' wives, her answer was, "This is just the way God made me. I just talk a lot and say things people don't like to hear." Indeed. Her talk caused no small degree of trouble within our congregation, and she was confronted on numerous occasions. Such sentiments about communication are precisely what Solomon wrote about in Proverbs 18:2: "A fool takes no pleasure in understanding, but only in expressing his opinion." I'm sure none of us wants to be described by those words. Still, how often do the best of us participate in thoughtless conversations and later realize we said things that shouldn't characterize a Christian—maybe we unwittingly gossiped about someone, slandered another church member, or unjustly criticized our pastor and only realize it after later reflection. Or, worse yet, we never realize it. If we're honest, it's easy to do, and we've all done it. In an effort at humor, I recently made an off-color comment to a friend about another person. The next day I reflected on what I'd said and realized my comment was mean-spirited and cutting. I called him back and apologized for making such a stupid remark. That's what I mean by loose talk.

As a big talker, and one who many years ago might have best been categorized as a "loose talker," one of the best lessons I've learned from older, wiser believers is simple and profound: think before you speak. Weigh your words, and learn to ask questions consistent with Acts 4:29: "Will this build up that other person or tear them down?" "Will it encourage or unnecessarily discourage them?" "Will my words honor God?" "I know God hears everything I say, so am I ashamed for him to hear me say this?" "Am I talking just to be talking—talking because silence feels awkward—or is there a good

---

23. David Powlison, *Speaking the Truth in Love: Counsel in Community* (Greensboro, NC: New Growth Press, 2005), 84.

purpose for what I'm about to say?" "Am I talking so the conversation can remain centered on me?"

Ask God to help you think about your talk this way, and his Spirit will help you grow into a more God-glorifying, others-centered talker.

## HOPE FOR TROUBLED TALKERS?

So far, what we've discussed sounds like a massive heap of bad news. Jesus said we will be justified or condemned by our words, and there are many ways we may sin, from slander and gossip to lying and careless talk. Thus, we must learn that the gospel transforms our sinful talk, enabling us to use words to convey grace and truth.

## MEMORY VERSE

*Let no corrupting talk come out of your mouth, but only as is good for building up, as fits the occasion, that it might give grace to those who hear.* (Eph. 4:29)

## QUESTIONS FOR GROUP DISCUSSION

1. Why might it be fitting to call slander and gossip "catastrophic cousins"? How are they related? How are they different? Why are they particularly troublesome for local churches?

2. How do gossip and slander relate to our natural tendency to enjoy stories?

3. Do you tend to be a critical person? If so, how does that reality affect those you criticize? How does the way you handle criticism shape the way you talk about others? How is Jesus's Golden Rule in Matthew 7:12 important here? What does Jesus mean when he says treating others the way you want to be treated "is the Law and the Prophets"?

4. Why is sarcasm such a problem in light of Jesus's command to love our neighbor as ourselves? When have you used sarcasm to cut others down and build yourself up?

5. When does the Bible say boasting is appropriate? Why is boasting such a subtle sin?

6. Is it ever right for a follower of Christ to lie? What about the prostitute Rahab? Did she sin by lying? What about Corrie ten Boom when she hid Jews from Nazis? Why is truth at the heart of the Christian faith?

7.  What is a "little lie"? Is it okay to tell a "little lie"? How does telling the truth align us with God?

8.  Does your anger tend to manifest more like a volcano or a simmering pot? Why are both problematic?

9.  Why is it particularly dangerous to talk when we're angry? What can you do to bridle your tongue when you get angry?

10. How do the Israelites illustrate the deep sinfulness of grumbling? How does the New Testament speak to that problem? How does grumbling relate to God's sovereignty?

11. How is grumbling really an expression of discontentment? How is it a form of spiritual adultery, and how does Puritan Thomas Boston parse it?

12. Why can't you judge the motives of others? Read and discuss Matthew 7:1–5. What is the picture Jesus is painting for us?

13. Does the Bible give warrant for Christians to use profanity? What does profanity have to do with God? What does profanity say about the condition of our hearts?

14. Why shouldn't you admire people who "tell it like it is"? Do you tend to "tell it like it is"? When does that kind of talk become sinful talk?

## FOR FURTHER READING AND STUDY

- *The Weight of Your Words: Measuring the Impact of What You Say* (Moody, 1998) by Joseph M. Stowell
- *Uprooting Anger: Biblical Help for a Common Problem* (P&R, 2005) by Robert D. Jones
- *A Small Book about a Big Problem: Meditations on Anger, Patience, and Peace* (New Growth Press, 2018) by Edward T. Welch
- *The Secret of Contentment* (P&R, 2010) by William B. Barcley
- *The Rare Jewel of Christian Contentment* (Banner of Truth, 1964) by Jeremiah Burroughs

# CHAPTER 4

# THE HEALING
# BALM IN
# OUR MOUTH

*A word fitly spoken is like apples of gold in a setting of silver.* (Prov. 25:11)

*Tonight, I ask for your prayers for all those who grieve, for the children whose worlds have been shattered, for all whose sense of safety and security has been threatened. And I pray they will be comforted by a power greater than any of us, spoken through the ages in Psalm 23: "Even though I walk through the valley of the shadow of death, I fear no evil, for you are with me."*
—President George W. Bush to the United States on the evening of
September 11, 2001

"Are you a clergyman?" the state trooper asked me. "Yes, sir, I'm a pastor," I replied. "Can you come with me, then? We need your help. How long have you been a pastor?" I wasn't certain of the kind of help he sought, but it sounded like no ordinary request, and these were not ordinary circumstances. "Yes, I'll help. I've been a full-time pastor for two weeks," I said.

His eyebrows raised, "Wow. Well, you're about to get some hard experience."

Three days earlier, the worst tornado outbreak in U.S. history had cut a deadly path across central Alabama, where my family had moved two weeks earlier to answer God's call for me to serve as a local church pastor. An EF5 twister had decimated the community north of Birmingham, where our team was helping dig through the aftermath.

The trooper led me into a small metal building that had once been a utility shed. It was one of the few things left standing in this small town and now functioned as a staging office for rescue/cleanup efforts. Seated at a flimsy card table were two sets of grandparents. The "hard experience" I was about to get involved telling them that rescuers had found their son, son-in-law, and two young grandchildren—the storm dealt their house a direct hit, and the funnel had swept them away. All were dead.

I never had to do that in the seminary classroom.

The trooper introduced me as a local Baptist pastor who had some news to tell them and then left me with four people I had met 90 seconds earlier.

Doubtless, the presence of clergy as a news bearer tipped them off as to the nature of the looming message. Through tears of my own, and with a Sahara-dry mouth and a stammering tongue, I managed to deliver the dark communiqué as the trooper had asked. All four wept deep, bitter tears. I sat in silence, weeping with them. My first act as a full-time pastor left me feeling like a rookie being asked to pitch game seven of the World Series.

I said nothing until one of the men looked at me and asked the inevitable existential question: "Pastor, what should we think of a god who would allow such a thing to happen? Not just to us, but to so many? Is there a god out there who can comfort us?"

Tornadoes killed 263 that day in Alabama. One of the strongest wiped out this entire family—bodies of the daughter, daughter-in-law, and another grandchild had already been recovered. What human words would suffice to provide comfort amid so much carnage?

I paused for several seconds, my hands trembling, toggling through all the possible things I could say in answer to his question. I knew there was a time to simply be present as moral support for hurting people, but now I had to say something because these hurting people were looking for answers. I opted for a paraphrase of inspired words, spoken slowly, carefully communicated: "I don't know why this happened, because the Lord doesn't always give us reasons why specific things happen in our lives—even tragic things. But I do know the kind of God who allowed this—he is a God Scripture calls sovereign and good, a God who is righteous in all his ways and kind in all his works. A God whom we can trust wholly, even when what we see doesn't make sense. He is the God of all comfort who is near us in times of darkness such as these. He is a God who knows all about suffering the loss of a child, for he sent his own Son to be the Savior of a fallen world plagued by tornadoes and death."

I prayed with them, joined in a tear-saturated embrace with each one individually, and rejoined the men from my church who remained hard at work in a field that was once a small subdivision, the scene of several deaths. For the rest of the day—and for several weeks that followed—I wondered if I was able to comfort them at all. My prayer for that brief but intense encounter was that God would use my stumbling paraphrase of his Word—even in a small way—as a tiny bit of light amid what was, no doubt, one of the darkest days that family had ever faced. Words kill, yes, but they can also heal.

## WORDS OF GRACE ARE WORDS OF LIFE

As chapters two and three have shown, Scripture bristles with warnings about how sinful our tongues are, how often we use words as a wounding, killing sword. But for followers of Christ, it doesn't have to be that way. Most fundamentally, God's Word itself is good news. He created us in his own image; we are fallen, dead, captive to sin's dark night; but now we are being redeemed by the grace of God in Christ, and our talk may reflect the good news that the gospel proclaims. Paul gets at this in Ephesians 4:29, a verse we've already encountered, but has served as a key passage for me these past few years as I've battled talk-related sins: "Let no corrupting talk come out of your mouths, but only as is good for building up, as fits the occasion, that it might give grace to those who hear."

Our tongues destroy, but they also have the potential to give life. That day in Alabama, I sought to give a measure of gospel comfort by quoting God's healing Word. On the evening of 9/11, U.S. President George W. Bush sought to comfort a grieving nation after Muslim terrorists killed thousands of Americans in New York, Pennsylvania, and Washington. He quoted Psalm 23 and asked the nation to petition the God who inspired it for streams of mercy. President Bush sought to comfort a reeling people with his words. As Christians, whether we are pastors or laypeople, we are called to do likewise.

Comforting words are gospel words. That's what Paul is telling the church at Ephesus in Ephesians 4:29—don't use your tongue to communicate bad news, but to express words that are commensurate with the gospel—words that heal, words of grace. Is there good news for our troubled talk? Yes, there is, and the context of Ephesians 4:29 gives us hope that our talk can be transformed.

Paul, as is his practice, gives three chapters of doctrine and then he pivots in Ephesians 4:1 he to three chapters of practical application, establishing how Christians are supposed to live in light of the gospel: "I therefore, a prisoner for the Lord, urge you to walk in a manner worthy of the calling to which you have been called." The manner in which he urges believers to walk is everything following 4:1, including 4:29, about how we are to talk. But how can depraved sinners talk in such a way to build up others? Because of what has happened in the first three chapters of Ephesians. Chapter one establishes all the spiritual blessings Christians have in Christ: they have been chosen (1:4, 11), adopted as sons and daughters into God's family (redeemed by the blood of Christ (1:7a), forgiven of all sins (1:7b), given an eternal inheritance (1:11), justified by faith and sealed by the Holy Spirit, who has come to live inside all who believe (1:13–14).

In Ephesians 2, Paul tells about the way we were before—dead in our trespasses and walking with the world, the flesh, and the Devil—before we were saved by grace alone through faith alone in Christ alone (2:8). He proceeds in chapter two to discuss the unity of the church, then in chapter three celebrates our union with Christ and the implications of that reality. In short, the Christian has been redeemed by the death and resurrection of Jesus Christ, has been indwelt by his Holy Spirit, and is able now to live in a manner worthy of the gospel.

Here's the good news for our talk: because of regeneration and the indwelling Spirit, our tongues are no longer captive to sin and death. No longer are we slaves to all those forms of talk we fleshed out in chapter 3. We are free to use our tongues selflessly as agents of healing, proclamation, and encouragement—words of life, consistent with the new life we've been given in Christ. A new heart means a new mouth.

Ephesians 4:29 guides us in how we should now talk, how we can refrain from using words of death and also begin speaking words of life. Words of life reflect the beauty of the gospel; they comfort, they are careful, they are centered on others, and they encourage and build up at the right time.

## WORDS OF LIFE REFLECT
## GOSPEL BEAUTY

Have there ever been more beautiful words written than these: "For our sake he made him to be sin who knew no sin, so that in him we might become the righteousness of God" (2 Cor. 5:21)? It is perhaps Scripture's pithiest expression of the gospel. The sinless Savior took our sin and gave us his righteousness. Extraordinary words. Seismic words. Words of grace. Those words enable believers to refrain from words that are sword thrusts and put in their place words that infuse our conversations with grace and life.

Paul, in Colossians 4:6, instructs us to use our words in this manner: "Let your speech always be gracious, seasoned with salt, so that you may know how you ought to answer each person." Words of grace are just that—in both substance and tone, they reflect a heart that has been changed by the mercy of God. They are wise and arresting, "salty" in the sense of a Christian's calling to be salt and light (Matt. 5:13–16). Yes, that does include evangelism, but that's not all Paul has in mind here. John Calvin writes:

> [Paul] requires suavity of speech, such as may allure the hearers by its profitableness, for he does not merely condemn communications that are openly wicked or impious, but also such as are worthless and idle. Hence he would have them seasoned with salt.... For [Paul] reckons as tasteless everything that does not edify.[1]

How do words of life reflect the gospel? At the heart of the gospel is Christ's selflessness: he laid down his life so that his people could have life. In the same way, words of life reflect the gospel by selflessly building up and centering on others.

---

1.  John Calvin, *Calvin's Commentaries, Volume XXI: Galatians, Ephesians, Colossians, 1 & 2 Timothy, Titus, Philemon*, trans. William Pringle (Grand Rapids: Baker, 1999), 225–26.

## WORDS OF GRACE
## ARE OTHERS-CENTERED

Because the gospel sets us free from self-love and motivates us to love others, words of grace are intrinsically others-centered, because grace is others-centered. God calls us to cultivate humility, which necessarily makes a wide berth for the other person. How many of our conversations with others focus on us? How often are we halfway listening to the other person, really just formulating our next words, merely waiting for even the slightest opening to speak? Or, if we're on the other side of such a monologue, we can feel a bit like the boyfriend musing over his loquacious girlfriend in Toby Keith's hit country-western song "I Wanna Talk about Me":

> We talk about your dreams and we talk about your schemes,
> Your high school team and your moisturizer cream,
> We talk about your nanna up in Muncie, Indiana
> We talk about your grandma down in Alabama
> You know talking about you makes me grin
> But every now and then
>
> I wanna talk about me,
> Wanna talk about I
> Wanna talk about number one on my radar
> What I think, what I like, what I know, what I want, what I see
> I like talking about you, you, you, usually
> But occasionally
> I wanna talk about me

Sure, I like to talk about me, yet Paul calls us to build others up, to love our neighbor with our words. Chattering ceaselessly about ourselves can make others feel worthless. Jesus had a way of talking to others that put them at ease. In John 4, the woman at the well seemed at ease talking to the Lord, even when they were discussing her sinful life. Most of the talk was about her, as Jesus asked personal questions.

In 2 Corinthians 5:15, Paul says Christ has liberated us from self-centered living: "and he died for all, that those who live might no longer live for themselves but for him who for their sake died and was raised." Our conversations cannot be grace-driven if they include only words about me—my thoughts, my desires, my life, my dreams, my past, my present, my future.

My wife once tried to build a relationship with a woman in our church, but could get nowhere, because their conversations never got past the other lady. My wife would ask her, "How is your family?" She'd say, "Fine." My wife would ask her about the kids, and the lady would answer with only information about her family and herself. My wife met with her for coffee on more than one occasion, and she never asked my wife a personal question. No questions about her family, her background, her walk with the Lord, nothing. Lisa got to know much about the other lady, but it was a runaway monologue. My wife eventually gave up, not because she wanted to talk about herself, but because the relationship was one-sided. The soil of communication was too shallow for a genuine relationship to germinate and thrive.

Jesus Christ, the Lord of the universe, asked questions of those whom he encountered, including his disciples. His conversations were not one-sided. He did not dominate others with an avalanche of self-centered words. He asked questions and listened well. We must do the same if we would communicate in a way fully in line with God's grace.

Where possible, we should serve others with our conversations. Ask thoughtful, personal questions. And listen well.

## WORDS OF GRACE COMFORT

Comfort is an oft-needed, seldom-found commodity, but should be more prevalent among God's people. In 2 Corinthians 1:4, Paul says the God of all comfort "comforts us in all affliction, so that we may be able to comfort those who are in any affliction with the comfort with which we ourselves are comforted by God." The people of God are called to comfort one another, which includes comforting talk. It's what I was attempting to do for the heartbroken family amid their unthinkable loss in the tornado.

My wife and I had never been able to relate to the many families around us that suffered through failed pregnancies until our first son died in Lisa's womb after five months in fall 1999. We were planning on naming him after my distant cousin, Brooks Robinson, a baseball legend, in hopes God would give him that same baseball gene. In the years that followed, we were amazed at how many friends came to us for counsel and encouragement after losing a child in utero.

I had never really been able to relate to fellow pastors whose ministries exploded like Mount Vesuvius until mine did three years into my first pastorate. Previously, the best I could do was offer some Reformed-sounding platitudes featuring the Puritans, Spurgeon, and maybe Corrie ten Boom, assuring them that these saints suffered and we must too. But my words fell with a thud; I knew not of what I spoke.

Scripture itself is a healing balm. The psalms, for example, provide a strong foundation for a theology of comforting words in dozens of places, including Psalm 23, Psalm 37, and Psalm 112, among others. Jesus comforted his disciples as his death, resurrection, and ascension loomed: "In the world you will have tribulation. But take heart; I have overcome the world" (John 16:33).

In the wake of Eliphaz's proclamation that Job's sin demonstrates his lack of a fear of God, Job got fed up with their un-pastoral care and concluded, "I have heard many such things; miserable comforters are you all." Sometimes we can say that right thing at the wrong time or in the wrong way. As we have already seen, Job's friends are perhaps Scripture's best illustration of good theology wrongly applied, spoken at the wrong time in the wrong way. Eliphaz the Temanite, in particular, had a sound theological understanding of sin but only made his friend more miserable with its application. As part of "walking in a manner worthy of the calling to which you have been called" (Eph. 4:1), Paul condemns "unwholesome talk" that tears others down. Instead, Christians should seek to build others up: "Let no unwholesome talk come out of your mouths, but only such as as good for building others up, as fits the occasion." How do we build others up? By encouraging, exhorting, correcting, comforting—using our words in ways that fit the occasion.

In the wake of the Alabama tornadoes, that family needed words of comfort. Recently, a pastor friend became upset at his church and called me, vowing to quit ministry altogether after 25 years of faithful service. After two hours of conversation, my friend realized his desire to quit arose from false expectations and a sinful desire for comfort. That was not my assumption when I picked up the phone, but as we applied Scripture and discussed that situation and as I sought to calm his heart and mind with loving, grace-driven words, it became clear his motives were mixed. Today, he remains as pastor of that church. He needed words of encouragement and exhortation—both words of grace.

Words of grace are not the same as flattery—in fact, they are the opposite. Scripture has a pointed assessment of flattery. Passages such as Proverbs

29:5, Romans 16:18, and 1 Thessalonians 2:5 expose flattery's self-centered underside: we build others up with the aim of making much of ourselves. If I tell a young, well-known writer that his prose is every bit as good as Hemingway's because I want him to like me and work for me, I have (1) lied (he's no Hemingway) and (2) used highly exaggerated words to get him to think favorably of me. I want to reel him in for my team and have used inflated words as the bait. Philippians 2:3 asks that Christians "do nothing from selfish ambition or conceit, but in humility count others as more significant than ourselves." Self-centeredness sits at the heart of flattery and, really, merely wants to talk about me.

Even difficult conversations can build up all parties involved in the dialogue—provided we are careful what we say and how we say it. The elder who sat me down and told me I was undermining my ministry with my out-of-control talk was being a friend. He used hard words, but spoke them graciously. It helped our friendship. Another friend once sat me down and gently but firmly told me I that I was seriously addicted to work and that it was affecting my family. He was right, and it helped me to make much-needed adjustments in my work schedule. Today, he's one of my dearest friends in the ministry. He commended me for my work ethic and conscientiousness, but then told me it was too much. The way he handled that conversation told me I could trust him. More on that in chapter five.

## WORDS OF GRACE AFFIRM

When we are only cynical or critical toward others, it's a troubling sign that there's trouble in our hearts. Are we only cranky in how we relate to others? Do we consider most other people misfits or morons? John Piper says a reticence to praise others is evidence of a soul sickness in us: "When our mouths are empty of praise for others, it is probably because our hearts are full of love for self."[2] Piper cites this penetrating passage by C. S. Lewis in *Reflections on the Psalms*:

2. Sam Crabtree, *Practicing Affirmation: God-Centered Praise of Those Who Are Not God* (Wheaton, IL: Crossway, 2011), Kindle edition, location 66. I unreservedly recommend this work for a much fuller study of why and how we should affirm others in a manner that is gloriously biblical. The author tackles issues beyond the scope of this section, such as whether we should affirm unbelievers and how we should assess our hearts when we crave good affirmation.

The world rings with praise—lovers praising their mistresses, readers their favorite poet, walkers praising the countryside, players praising their favorite game—praise of weather, wines, dishes, actors, motors, horses, colleges, countries, historical personages, children, flowers, mountains, rare stamps, rare beetles, even sometimes politicians or scholars. I had not noticed how the humblest, and at the same time most balanced and capacious, minds praised most, while the cranks, misfits, and malcontents praised least.[3]

But don't we all crave the applause of men? Won't we stir up pride when we build others up? Won't we risk flattery and encourage idolatry? Not if we take the Bible seriously. When we praise them for the right reasons, then we are praising God, because we are praising his image-bearers. James 3:9 speaks of how it's wrong that, with the same tongue, we bless God and curse people made in his image. I think it's a valid inference that we can praise people at fitting times because they are his image-bearers. Proverbs 31:30 says that a woman who fears the Lord is to be praised, and I think it's good and right to assume that we can praise men who fear God as well. And what will every saint hear from the Lord on judgment day? "Well done, good and faithful servant" (Matt. 25:21, 23). In affirming other believers, we are simply affirming the good work God has done and is doing in them (1 Cor. 4:7; 15:10).

I think affirmation is part of what Solomon is driving at in Proverbs 25:11 when he says a word fitly spoken (at the right time) is like apples of gold in a setting of silver. It doesn't encourage me when people say, "Preacher, that was a great sermon." But it does encourage me when someone says, "You've really grown as a preacher. Your sermons are getting clearer and more concise. It's great to see the Lord grow you in this way." That's encouraging, because I'm always looking for ways to grow as a preacher, and I'm constantly praying toward that end.

Space and scope forbid multiplying biblical illustrations, but here's one: after he survived the lion's den without a scratch, Daniel honors God by affirming Darius for hurrying to the scene the morning after Daniel had been fed to the lions to see if God had rescued his man: "Oh king, live forever" (Dan. 6:21). Sam Crabtree writes of this instance: "God is not dishonored, for if king Darius lives forever, it will be God who brings it to pass. God gets

---

3.  Ibid., location 127.

the credit for being the one able to do the work.... God is glorified in us when we affirm the work he has done and is doing in others."[4]

Affirmation can bring health to relationships, especially when they've been rubbed raw by criticism—even necessary criticism—or bickering. This notion particularly applies to parents of teenagers. I am raising three teens and often need to admonish them toward maturity, which doesn't always sit well with them. I've found that affirming them as much as possible helps them to remember that when I do correct them, I am functioning as a loving parent who sees good things in them and wants what's best for them. Last year, my oldest son struggled academically, but got a job on his own, worked hard, and excelled. While discussing how he'll seek to improve as a student this year, I commended him for how he'd found a job and had demonstrated a strong work ethic, one that honors God (1 Cor. 10:31; Col. 3:23). As I've found areas in which to commend him, I've noticed that he takes my critique and correction with a far better attitude. Recently he even told me, "I know you get on me about these things because you love me. I'm sorry I don't always handle it well. I guess that's part of maturing that we always talk about." Those words encouraged me in return.

Jesus was not compelled to save us because he owed us something. He was compelled to save us because of his love for us. By grace we are saved, through faith. In the same way, affirmation of others is not a duty owed, but a generous expression of grace entirely consistent with the gospel.

## WORDS OF GRACE CONFRONT

Sometimes, the presence of sin means words of grace speak the truth in love by correcting or admonishing others. Proverbs 27:6 says, "Faithful are the wounds of a friend; profuse are the kisses of an enemy." Faithfulness to proclaiming the grace of God in Christ demands it: "Declare these things; exhort and rebuke with all authority" (Titus 2:15).

Jesus confronted in a way that was consistent with his being full of grace and truth (John 1:14). His rebukes reflected both. For example, look at how Jesus confronted the misguided young ruler in Mark 10:17–27 who told the Lord, "Teacher, I have kept all these (laws of God) from my youth." Jesus looked at him, "loved him and said to him, 'You lack one thing: go, sell all that you have and give to the poor, and you will have treasure in heaven;

4.   Ibid., location 143.

and come, follow me'" (Mark 10:21). The rich young man did not follow Jesus—he loved his money and possessions more than he loved God. But Jesus
loved him and spoke carefully with him in order to reveal the true motives of
his heart. He didn't debate the finer points of theology or tell the young man
how sick his heart really was; the Lord confronted him without compromise,
in a way that loved him.

Of course, Jesus in Matthew 18:15–20 provides the church with a formal
three-step way for Christians confronting and disciplining the sins of other
Christians within the context of the body. Church discipline is a means of
loving God and loving our neighbor because its goal is twofold: keep the
church pure and bring back the brother or sister who's straying in life or
doctrine. The goal of church discipline is not punitive; it's intended for res-
toration of the erring member. Confrontation, when carried out lovingly in
accord with Matthew 18 and 1 Corinthians 5, is an act of gospel-picturing
love.[5] After all, just a few verses before the section on church discipline in
Matthew 18, Jesus left the 99 and pursued the one lost sheep, bringing the
one back into the fold.

The elder of whom I spoke in the preface was putting this principle into
action—I had a blind spot, one that threatened my ministry, one that threatened to seriously undermine my Christian witness. And though his words
were not easy for me to hear at the time, he spoke them to me out of a desire
for my growth in Christ. In 1 Corinthians 13:6, Paul defines love, in part, as
rejoicing in the truth. Thus, if we would minister to those whom we love, we
must be truth-tellers, saying difficult things when necessary, but always in a
tone commensurate with the gospel and the love of Christ. We'll discuss in
much more detail how to navigate difficult discussions in the next chapter.

Yes, the tongue must be tamed, but our tongue can also serve as a healing balm to others. When we use our words to redeem, to build up, encourage, comfort, and even confront others lovingly, we fulfill Paul's mandate in
Ephesians 4:29.

---

5.   For a more expansive study of how God's love is shown through church discipline, I
     highly recommend Jonathan Leeman's book *The Church and the Surprising Offense of God's
     Love: Reintroducing the Doctrines of Church Membership and Discipline* (Wheaton, IL: Cross-
     way, 2010).

## MEMORY VERSES

*A word fitly spoken is like apples of gold in a setting of silver.* (Prov. 25:11)

*And he died for all, that those who live might no longer live for themselves but for him who for their sake died and was raised.* (2 Cor. 5:15)

*Therefore, if anyone is in Christ, he is a new creation. The old has passed away; behold, the new has come.* (2 Cor. 5:17)

## QUESTIONS FOR GROUP DISCUSSION

1. How can words give life to others in a way consistent with the gospel?

2. How does having a new heart and the indwelling Spirit change the way we talk? Why aren't we enslaved to old patterns of anger and old patterns of sinful talk? Look up 2 Corinthians 5:17. How does that verse apply to our communication?

3. Why is Ephesians 4:29 such an important verse for our transformed tongues? How do the first three chapters of Ephesians set up that verse and make it good news and not something we need to try to do in our own strength?

4. How many ways can we use our talk to build up others? How does it picture the gospel when we do?

5. Think about how you approach conversations with others, ranging from your church small group to one-on-one conversations. Do you tend to dominate them? Do you tend to talk over the other person? Do you ask questions about them and their lives, their thoughts, or do you tend to talk about yourself, your life, your thoughts, your dreams? Why is that contrary to the gospel?

6. What strategies can you take to make your conversations less centered on yourself and more focused on others?

7. In 2 Corinthians 1:3–4, Paul seems to want us to comfort others with our talk? When was the last time another Christian did that for you? What are some issues on which you feel comfortable giving help and comfort to other Christians?

8. How were Job's friends miserable comforters? How did they misapply and misuse sound doctrine? How is that instructive for us, especially when we fancy ourselves as having our "I's" dotted and "t's" crossed doctrinally?

9.  How can you affirm other Christians without flattering them or stirring up their sinful desire for affirmation? How do you take it when other believers affirm you? When might affirmation bleed over into flattery or man-centered "buttering up"?

10. Why is it loving to confront another Christian in his or her sin? When is a rebuke consistent with proclaiming grace?

11. Is church discipline as set forth in Matthew 18 and 1 Corinthians 5 vindictive and mean-spirited, or is it an expression of God's mercy and love? Have you seen church discipline done poorly or done well? How can we make certain our confrontation is consistent with Jesus who is full of grace and truth?

12. How and why does love rejoice with truth? How can you demonstrate this when you have to confront another believer in the church when they've sinned against you? How should you talk to them in a way that's both serious and loving?

## FOR FURTHER READING AND STUDY

- *Practicing Affirmation: God-Centered Praise of Those Who Are Not God* (Crossway, 2011) by Sam Crabtree
- *When People Are Big and God Is Small: Overcoming Peer Pressure, Codependency, and the Fear of Man* (P&R, 1997) by Edward T. Welch

# CHAPTER 5

# IT'S IN THE WAY
# WE TALK

*A soft answer turns away wrath, but a harsh word stirs up anger.* (Prov. 15:1)

*There ain't no good guy, there ain't no bad guy; there's only you and me, and we just disagree.* —British rock singer/songwriter Dave Mason

Over the years, I've taught college and high school classes on writing, and I love to begin with humorous examples of how not to write. Sometimes I ask students, "Did you know that a comma splice can lead to cannibalism?" I have them consider these two sentences: "Let's eat Grandma" and "Let's eat, Grandma." Sometimes, punctuation derails a well-worded sentence, but we usually only notice punctuation when it's faulty.

Or, headlines can skew our understanding. During the 1934 World Series, St. Louis Cardinals pitcher Dizzy Dean, one of baseball's all-time characters, was hit in the head by the ball while running the bases and feared lost for the entire series. The next day, this headline sat above the fold on *The*

*New York Times* sports page: "They X-Rayed My Head and Found Nothing." Dean pitched as scheduled and never quite lived down his empty head.

Tone can introduce the same kind of mixed messages into our conversations as poor punctuation or humorous headlines. We notice tone in the same way we hear that off-key choir member. Like the time I took a complaint to my high school baseball coach. I let him know, in no uncertain terms, that I was not thrilled that he had moved me out of the leadoff slot in our batting order. I assured him that I was not a number-three hitter, but a leadoff man. After all, my only real redeeming athletic qualities were decent speed, a good idea of the strike zone, and a penchant for making contact with the ball, attributes typically found in a leadoff hitter. I also reminded him that I'd been batting at the top of the lineup since I was in T-ball (It never occurred to me that this was likely due to the fact that my dad had often been my coach.)

That was 34 years ago, but I'll never forget his response: "You know, Jeff, the problem with you is I can't hear what you're saying to me because your attitude is talking so loud." My coach walked away, leaving me to ponder his pithy aphorism. It didn't take me long to interpret it: my disrespectful tone was keeping him from hearing my sincere—perhaps even valid—case as to why I could best help the team by batting atop the order.

It wasn't what I said that was the problem; it was the way I said it. Many of our communication issues aren't necessarily related to our selection of words but the tone in which we speak them. Here's an example: You're having a lively disagreement with your spouse over whether or not she should see a doctor about a lingering pain in her stomach. Which response would be more likely to promote a healthy dialogue?

"Listen to me, you're just being paranoid. There's nothing wrong with you."

Or:

"I hear what you're saying, and I can understand why you're worried, but until we see a doctor I'd encourage you to try not to be anxious about this."

Both communicate the same idea, but with different words and attitudes that convey different tones.

Or, you could tell her "Yes, you look great in that dress," using the exact same words but in two different ways. One would make her happy you've noticed; the other would insult her and perhaps even send her back to change the dress.

Here's another example: You're talking to a friend who has embraced a theological error or an ethical practice forbidden by Scripture. You could say, "How could you possibly buy into such idiotic nonsense?" But it would be better—and more Christlike—to use a strategy Costi Hinn calls "HMU—help me understand."[1] Then you'd ask something like, "Help me to understand why you've rejected the Bible's teaching on homosexuality" or "Help me to understand why you're attracted to Mormon teaching." The latter two statements are more loving. They are not dismissive and will likely lead to a calmer and perhaps more fruitful dialogue.

Proverbs 15:1 represents perhaps the best advice regarding tone in the entire Bible: "A soft answer turns away wrath, but a harsh word stirs up anger." Our Lord Jesus Christ models tone well in his encounter with the woman at the well in John 4. Even when Jesus tells her that he knows she is currently living with a man and has had five previous husbands, his tone is gentle and non-combative: "You are right in saying, 'I have no husband'; for you have had five husbands, and the one you now have is not your husband. What you have said is true" (vv. 17-18). Jesus's tone was gracious and uncondemning, yet he did not compromise the truth.

Often, our tone, our body language, or even our inadvertently insensitive way of phrasing things undermines good communication. Good communication tends to happen when tone is invisible. Good tone massages your words into the hearer's heart. Tone is like an umpire in baseball; umpires are at their best when no one notices them—when they are managing the game well and everything is going smoothly. It's when we begin to notice the wonky strike zone, or their strident response when a batter questions the call, that they become part of the game. In the same way, tone promotes smooth, godly communication when it's not a factor.

Tone is not just a small, pragmatic concern. From the highest levels of spiritual, national, and executive leadership, Solomon and the sages of Israel instruct the nation's royal sons toward gentle speech, a persuasive tongue, and situationally wise tones that build trust and persuade people—all because the speaker fears God, exercises self-control, and senses the need of the moment, consistent with Paul's instruction in Ephesians 4:[2]

---

1.  Costi Hinn, *God, Greed, and the (Prosperity) Gospel: How the Truth Overwhelms a Life Built on Lies* (Grand Rapids: Zondervan, 2019), 206.
2.  David "Gunner" Gundersen, "7 Secret Weapons in Ministry," https://davidagundersen. com/2016/05/16/seven-secret-weapons-in-ministry.

A gentle tongue is a tree of life,
but perverseness in it breaks the spirit.
(Prov. 15:4)

The heart of the wise makes his speech judicious
and adds persuasiveness to his lips.
(Prov. 16:23)

Gracious words are like a honeycomb,
sweetness to the soul and health to the body.
(Prov. 16:24)

With patience a ruler may be persuaded,
and a soft tongue will break a bone.
(Prov. 25:15)

Granted, the Bible doesn't use the word "tone," but it's clearly what Solomon and other writers of Scripture have in mind in some passages. In a well-known verse related to evangelism, Peter tells his readers not merely that they should always be ready to give a defense for the hope that lies within them. He also tells us the demeanor and attitude that should accompany gospel proclamation: "gentleness and respect."

But in your hearts honor Christ the Lord as holy, always being prepared to make a defense to anyone who asks you for a reason for the hope that is in you; yet do it with gentleness and respect. (1 Pet. 3:15)

If we owe it to unbelievers to handle them with gentleness and respect, how much more do we owe it to our brothers and sisters within the church? Paul commends this same adornment for our talk in Colossians 4:6, "Let your speech always be gracious, seasoned with salt, so that you may know how you ought to answer each person." In the ancient world, salt was used as a preservative for meat, helping to keep it from spoiling. Similarly, a Christian's speech must always promote purity rather than spiritual corruption. This necessarily requires that both our words and also the way we use them be handled with care.

## ANOTHER WORD FOR IT: HUMILITY

When I told a close pastor friend that I planned on including a chapter on tone in this book, he challenged me to define it biblically. Though those proverbs don't use the word, I think they cover it nicely, but after some reflection on my friend's question, I've realized what I mean by tone is really our need to march all of our words under the banner of a core biblical virtue: humility. Peter commends humility to elders and the entire body of Christ in 1 Peter 5:5b–6:

> Clothe yourselves, all of you, with humility toward one another, for "God opposes the proud but gives grace to the humble." Humble yourselves, therefore, under the mighty hand of God so that at the proper time he may exalt you.

If we follow Peter's admonition to seek humility in all our conversation, then tone will take care of itself, even as we participate in difficult, conflict-filled conversations that we'll deal with later in the chapter.

How does humility affect the way we talk to others? What is humility? I love John Calvin's words at the beginning of his *Institutes*, because I think they get at the key to planting seeds of humility in our own hearts: genuine wisdom consists in knowledge of God and knowledge of self. Humility is honestly assessing ourselves in light of God's holiness and our sinfulness. Humility is the opposite of pride, and pride is, to paraphrase and summarize the words of the Pharisee in Luke 18:9–13, the conviction that I am already humble, probably more humble than most other people.[3]

Humility improves our communication with others. We enter the conversation aware that we are sinners saved by grace, aware that God is holy, aware that we have not received what our sins deserve. Since we're not above others, we do not want to talk to them in ways we'd never want to be talked to. If we need to correct others, we'll do it in a way that reflects the grace of Jesus. If we need to scold, we will be careful, and while we may need to be firm, it won't be unkind or harsh. Consistent with Proverbs 15:1, we can speak firmly, but with grace, kindness, and humility.

In Galatians, Paul confronts the church at Galatia for flirting with another gospel and later stands down a fellow apostle, Peter, for caving in to

---

3. William P. Farley, *Gospel-Powered Humility* (Phillipsburg, NJ: P&R, 2011), 185.

legalism. His words are straight and pointed but do not come off as harsh
or unkind. It's clear that he's upset and is speaking plainly to Peter and the
Galatians, but his words are straightforward, not cutting or snarky: "I am astonished that you are so quickly deserting him who called you in the grace of
Christ and turning to a different gospel—not that there is another one, but
there are some who trouble you and want to distort the gospel of Christ" (Gal.
1:6–7) Then, Paul tells us he opposed Peter to his face, and he mentions their
hypocrisy—firm words, but there's obviously nothing sinful about his tone.
A gracious tone does not preclude a serious confrontation, but it does keep
it from boiling over into conflict and can lead to a deepened relationship.

The elders in my church recently confronted a young member who'd
fallen into gross sin. As we spoke to this member, I couldn't help but notice
the deep humility demonstrated by one of my fellow elders, Doug, who was
a longtime lead pastor before becoming a leader in our congregation. Doug
was serious and firm, but communicated to this young man how much he
loved him, how dangerous his lifestyle was for a professing Christian, and
how we wanted him to flee from his sin and into the arms of Jesus. He was
confronting serious sin and by no means abdicated his duty. But his tone was
so gracious that God used it to melt the heart of our erring member. Another
elder and I were deeply affected by his Christ-like humility.

I think there's always a fear, especially among Reformed Christians, that
treating others too graciously is akin to compromise, that speaking harshly
at a higher volume equals standing firm for the truth. I don't know why
that's true (maybe it's the fundamentalist impulse that lives in so many of
us), but I've been guilty of harboring that fear myself. As a pastor, I've realized that harshness is never the right way to approach other people, no
matter what they've done to us or the church, or no matter how justified we
may be in our anger or disappointment with their sin. And as Solomon so
well instructed the young men in Proverbs 15:1 ("A gentle word turns away
wrath"), harsh speech never leads to fruitful conversation or healthy results.

All our conversations ought to be motivated by the love of Christ, which
Paul beautifully exegetes in 1 Corinthians 13:1–7, a passage I've most often
encountered in cross-stitched pictures given as wedding gifts (I think my
wife and I received three such pictures when we exchanged nuptials) and
hung on our walls as beautiful decorative pieces—only to be ignored as we
yell at each other in the hallway. Verses 4 and 5 are particularly pertinent to
the way we talk with each other: "Love is patient and kind; love does not

envy or boast; it is not arrogant or rude. It does not insist on its own way; it is not irritable or resentful."

For me, this is what makes most forms of social media an inferior form of communication, especially when a nuanced theological, political, or cultural matter is being discussed. We should be extremely cautious in how we talk with each other on social media, in email, or through text messages. It's easy to unintentionally communicate a bad tone.

Our tone is particularly important in helping or hindering what I like to call "minefield conversations," which is why I have chosen to deal with them in the same chapter.

## TEN WAYS TO NAVIGATE MINEFIELD CONVERSATIONS

During World War II, Adolf Hitler's armies planted more than 1 million "Bouncing Betty" mines across Europe. They killed thousands of allied soldiers because they were small and difficult to detect. Difficult conversations often feel like trying to get through that mine-laced countryside without killing oneself. All of us know these "minefield" talks all too well. Those conversations with the boss with a hair-triggered temper, that talk with our teenager about a sketchy friend that seems certain to get ugly, that confrontation a pastor has with a church member because the church is disciplining her teenage son, that theological conversation at Christmas with your uncle who is a Jehovah's Witness, that impromptu talk about politics with a co-worker who is far on the other side from you on social issues. Minefield conversations, fraught with danger, are certain to get some relationship killed. If you don't keep your wits about you, each step—every word—could be the last you ever speak to one another. You've been there, and I have too.

These conversations also include those times you have to give a rebuke to a fellow believer. How do we deal with those minefield conversations? How can we give a necessary rebuke in a Christlike manner? How can you be firm but loving? Here are 10 important things to consider.

## 1. PREPARE YOURSELF SPIRITUALLY.

Pray and meditate on pertinent Scripture verses before you enter the conversation. Here's an example of how this has helped me: Recently, I had to sit down with a friend who had joined my church, but had become disgruntled with the leadership of our elders. I knew he was going to leave the church, and that he could also have a ferocious temper if you didn't handle him gently. As I drove to our meeting place, I meditated on Proverbs 15:1a ("A gentle word turns away wrath") and Matthew 12:36 ("I tell you, on judgment day people will give account for every careless word they speak"), and I prayed that God would give me the grace to obey the commands tacit in these verses, that I would remember this is my brother in Christ and not an enemy.

Since the trouble in our talk is really a matter of the heart (Matt. 12:34), then we must enter these conversations with our hearts properly prepared. Typically, when engaging in these conversations, I'll pray for God to make my heart right so that I'll have the right tone and avoid getting angry. My heart needs to be overwhelmed by God's grace, reminded what's at stake, and shown again how patient God has been with me.

In that conversation with my friend, there were a few tense moments because we both spoke frankly, but it went well overall and ended with both of us encouraging each other and agreeing that our friendship did not depend on me being his pastor or his attending our church. I agreed with some of his critiques and found them helpful, while disagreeing with others. In the end, I thought it would be best if his family found another church home, and I offered my assistance. His family found a solid church in our city and, by God's grace, we remain friends today. I don't think it would have gone nearly so well had I not sought to prepare my heart and resolve, by God's grace, not to use harsh words or become angry.

My wife and I agreed that had this conversation taken place just a few years ago, it probably would have ended quite differently because of my own anger and pride issues. Going into the conversation after Bible meditation and prayer helped to steel my resolve to have a firm but brotherly dialogue.

## 2. ASK THREE QUESTIONS.

The late Reformed theologian Roger Nicole was known for his graciousness, particularly in interacting with those who disagreed with his theology. God gave him a keen ability to maintain a Christ-like posture and use calm, God-honoring words in the midst of heated debate.

He suggested we ask three questions to help us to maintain a Christ-like bearing amid disagreements: (1) What do I owe the person who differs with me? (Rom. 13:7–10 is a good place to begin answering this question); (2) What can I learn from a person who differs from me?; and, (3) How can

I cope with the person who differs from me?[4] Carefully considering these questions will help us slay pride and selfishness that too often lies at the root of our nasty debates and quarrelsome conversations.

## 3. BEGIN WITH THE MOST CHARITABLE JUDGMENT POSSIBLE.

Do your best to set a positive tone. Nothing circumvents communication like a conversation that begins with heat, continues with heat, and eventually (often quickly) grows into an anger-filled wildfire. If you begin with calm words that arise out of charitable judgment, this will help to relax both you and also your conversation partner.

For example, let's say you're confronting a fellow church member about the sin of gossip. You wouldn't want to start with, "Why in the world have you been saying such awful, ridiculous, slanderous things about me?" Even if you are pretty certain they're guilty and the things they said about you were awful, ridiculous, and slanderous, it'll be better to start the conversation with something like, "I'd like to talk with you about something you supposedly said about me that has been communicated back to me. Now, I want you to know that I'm by no means assuming you said it or meant ill by it, but I wanted to speak with you about it directly to be certain—It may have been misheard or misunderstood." Consistent with Christ's Golden Rule, you want others to assume your innocence, so do the same to them.

## 4. AS MUCH AS POSSIBLE, CHECK YOUR EMOTIONS AT THE DOOR.

Keep a tight rein on this particular stallion, for it can run away from you in a hurry. By the time you get it bridled and back in the barn, the damage may be substantial. Unbridled emotions are probably the most common match that lights the fuse that dynamites our conversations. God has made us emotional people, so emotion is not a bad thing—not always—but raw, unchecked emotion in a difficult conversation is often the road to nowhere.

4. Roger Nicole, "How to Deal with Those Who Differ from Us" in David W. Bailey, *Speaking the Truth in Love: The Life & Legacy of Roger Nicole* (Birmingham, AL: Solid Ground Christian Books, 2006), 184.

Unhinged emotions make you want to walk out and slam the door. They make you want to build a logical argument and shove it down their throat. They make you want to give them the cold shoulder. They tempt you to just absorb perceived mistreatment and move on, vowing to be done with them.

You want to respond in a manner that's controlled. You want to avoid responding with bare emotion. In a conversation that has potential for heated conflict, it's important to pray for genuine humility and ask the other person questions like, "Before we talk about how I think you've wronged me, I want to hear you out. Please be specific and tell me how I may have unintentionally hurt you."[5] This will elicit far better results and may lead to a God-honoring dialogue in a way that out-of-control emotions never could. This type of response could be the starting point for needed reconciliation.

Here's an example: I have a relative who is also a pastor, but from a different theological tradition than mine. Many years ago, he wanted to debate the doctrine of election with me, basically in Old West style as in Wild Bill Hickok and Wyatt Earp with revolvers at ten paces. In one of my better moments, driven 100 percent by God's grace, I told him, "I'll be glad to show you why I think the Bible teaches election and predestination. After all, I don't want to believe something if it's not biblical. Let's get our Bibles and I'll show you. Then, I want to hear why you don't think the doctrine is biblical and why you think it'd be better for me not to believe it." We talked for three hours, and while we still didn't agree on everything, he thanked me for what he felt was an edifying Bible study together. My relative expressed his objections graciously, and I listened without interrupting him. We avoided a relational blowup, and our friendship deepened. I came to understand him and his objections to this doctrine more clearly. Years later, he remains unconvinced of my view of God's sovereignty in salvation, but we enjoy a warm, collegial relationship.

## 5. KEEP A CLOSE WATCH ON YOUR BODY LANGUAGE.

It's not always your words or even the way you use them that stir up a hornet's nest within a conversation. Sometimes, it's your tone, as discussed earlier in this chapter, or it might be your bodily demeanor that adds unintend-

5. Ken Sande, *The Peacemaker: A Biblical Guide to Resolving Personal Conflict* (Grand Rapids: Baker, 2004), 169.

ed heat or an ungracious shape to your words. Ask your spouse or a close friend to help you detect tone or body language issues you may be unaware of. You may be sending others the wrong message unintentionally. In Psalm 101:5b, David warns, "Whoever has a haughty look and an arrogant heart I will not endure." "Haughty look" refers to demeanor. An arrogant look arises from an arrogant heart, and God will countenance neither.

My wife once pointed out that I tended to flair my nostrils during a contentious conversation and would also contort my face in such a way that I appeared to be angry and dismissive of the other person. Or, I would shake my head slightly while the other person was talking. Not exactly the way to foster gracious, helpful dialogue. I also looked angry when I preached, she said. I've tried to be conscious about softening my face while in the pulpit. I've come to realize that serious and angry are not nearly the same thing. Mary Beeke points out how significant our nonverbal communications can be:

> Tone of voice and facial expressions are huge factors. They express patience, tolerance, kindness, and happiness—or a lack thereof. When mom says, "Come here, Brian," her tone can convey either irritation or cheerfulness. When I am around a person with indomitable cheerfulness, I am uplifted; I feel safe, accepted, and comfortable in his or her presence. Wouldn't it be great if we all had that effect on each other? If we wish to improve our communication skills, this is the area to begin with that will make the most impact. By simply being aware of how we sound and our impact on others, we can take steps to change. It might involve dealing with underlying issues, but that is another subject. If we shore up the self-discipline it takes to be cheerful, our emotions may just follow along.[6]

We need to keep our wits such that we are aware of our posture, facial expressions, and the like. Like tone, body language can short-circuit dialogue, even if our words are careful.

---

6. Mary Beeke, *The Law of Kindness: Serving with Heart and Hands* (Grand Rapids: Reformation Heritage, 2007), 180–81.

## 6. SOFTEN YOUR LANGUAGE.

Avoid harsh, judgmental language or attitudes. Avoid emotive language. Intentionally use gracious, non-combative words. Remember Proverbs 15:1, "A soft answer turns away wrath, but a harsh word stirs up anger." Another important bit of biblical wisdom appears in Proverbs 12:18: "rash words are like sword thrusts, but the tongue of the wise brings healing."

For example, I had two conversations recently with my teenage son, one modeled what I'm aiming for here; the other was not one of my better parenting moments. In the first, we were talking about how and when he could use our car. I told him, "Please ask us when you want to use it, and unless there's a good reason why you can't, I'll probably say yes. I know you're a careful driver, and I trust you, but just make sure you ask and tell us where you're going and roughly how long you'll be gone. Then we'll be able to make a good decision." Our conversation was pleasant, and he was amenable to my words.

The second conversation, not so much. One of his younger siblings told me that he's been breaking the speed limit considerably during a recent drive to a fast food place. I didn't hesitate to hurl accusations and invectives at him. I told him that he'd been driving like a fool and how dangerous that was. I told him that I was tempted to suspend his driving privileges altogether. He was not happy with me, and I wasn't happy with him. He tried to tell me that his younger brother had misread the speedometer, but I kept cutting him off. My inner attorney was on the defense and in quite a nasty fashion. When he tried to ask me questions, I was defensive that he would even presume to question me, and I told him so. Needless to say, thanks to my accusatory tone and assumptions of guilt, our relationship suffered from that conversation. I totally blew it and sought his forgiveness.

Learn from my negative experience and be clear, constructive, and persuasive. Avoid defensive words and a defensive tone. That was a huge mistake I made in the latter conversation. The first conversation was much better because we spoke with humility and kindness that de-escalated the fight.

Paul models well gracious speech in a hostile setting in his dialogue with Agrippa in Acts 26:3. Paul has appealed the reason for his arrest to Caesar and stands before Agrippa, the great-grandson of Herod the Great. Paul's opening statement is pure Christlike *détente*: "I consider myself fortunate that it is before you, King Agrippa, I am going to make my defense today against all the accusations of the Jews, especially because you are familiar with all the customs and controversies of the Jews. Therefore, I beg you to listen to me patiently." Agrippa is clearly affected by Paul's careful words, concluding the apostle's defense by admitting, "In a short time would you persuade me to be a Christian?" (Acts 26:28) before rendering a plainly worded verdict: "This man is doing nothing to deserve death or imprisonment" (Acts 26:31). The old aphorism captures it well: "You catch more flies with honey than with vinegar."

## 7. SEEK CLARITY AND USE "HELPER WORDS."

Make sure you understand what the other person is saying. A few years ago, I was counseling a soon-to-be-married couple with serious communication problems that had led them to heated conflict. One particularly ugly fight started when he made an off-handed comment about her mother that he intended as a compliment. She took it as an insult, and fireworks followed. A lack of clarity led things in the wrong direction.

Ken Sande, in his outstanding book *The Peacemaker: A Biblical Guide to Resolving Personal Conflict*, defines clarity as "the process of making sure you understand what the other person is saying."[7] Clarity necessarily involves asking questions. Do it graciously. Seek clarity by asking or saying things like:[8]

"Are you saying…?"

"Tell me more about…"

"Can you give me a specific example…?"

"I'm a little confused about…"

"Here's what I understand you to be saying… Is that correct or am I off base?"

Seeking clarity shows the other person that you care about hearing their concern accurately. It's a good way to signal them that you're listening—more

7. Sande, *The Peacemaker*, 178.
8. Ibid.

on that in chapter six. I've found when I seek clarification, the person with whom I'm having a difficult conversation will sometimes begin to soften their tone or demeanor. It helps establish trust and often leads to a conversation that brings more light and less heat, because they know I'm genuinely trying to hear them out.

John Crotts provides much-needed help through the use of what he calls "gracious helper words." Using these words can help you avoid sounding unreasonable, harsh, arrogant, authoritarian or self-righteous. Here's what he means by "gracious helper words":

> Incorporate words and phrases into your dialogue designed to remind you of the need to be more gracious and to be a conduit of kindness. Expressions such as "I think," "it seems," or "from my perspective" acknowledge that you are aware you lack omniscience. While everyone else knows that you don't know everything, it is good for the people you address to hear you affirm that you don't know everything... Regardless of how often you are right, no one is always right. While you may be certain about many biblical truths, when you discuss them you should use humble phrases to genuinely help you to remain humble and further the conversation.[9]

Other words he recommends are "It *seems* like this is the way it is" or "It *seems* like this is what the verse is saying" or "*From my perspective,* that seems to be the direction to go." These words are affective, particularly in difficult or awkward conversations, because they convey humility and acknowledge our limitations. We avoid sounding harsh, authoritarian, or doctrinaire. These words could help guide the conversation in a better direction.[10]

## 8. REMEMBER THE GRACE OF GOD YOU'VE RECEIVED SO YOU'RE ABLE TO GIVE GRACE TO THE OTHER PERSON.

This is what the gospel does: it sets us free to treat every fellow saved sinner as an equal. We must remember that we've received grace upon grace upon

---

9.   John Crotts, *Graciousness: Tempering Truth with Love* (Grand Rapids: Reformation Heritage, 2018), Kindle edition, location 1265.

10.  Ibid.

grace, grace that God continues to pour into our lives every single day. Once a believer realizes how much he's received from the Lord, then he is in a position to breathe grace into his communication with others.

I briefly examined the parable of the unforgiving servant (Matt. 18:21–35) in chapter one. Remember the incredibly important lesson Jesus taught there: we have been forgiven an infinite debt of sin through the atoning death of Jesus Christ, so must now be quick to give grace to others. That enables us to handle difficult conversations in a gospel-driven way.

## 9. POSTURE YOURSELF AS A FRIEND, NOT AN ENEMY.

This is particularly vital if you are debating matters of theology, culture, or politics. It makes a profound difference if we assume the posture of a friend and not an enemy. Too many theological disagreements at least insinuate that the opposing side is so wrong on an issue that their Christian faith is probably not genuine. Of course that may be true when we are debating a matter that is the difference between heresy and orthodoxy such as at the Council of Nicaea in 325 when the Arians argued that there was a time when Jesus "was not."

But most of our debates are not matters that spell the difference between true Christianity and false. And when we are talking to fellow Christians, we should not view brothers and sisters in Christ as our enemies. This is true even when confronting a fellow believer about his sins. As Paul admonishes in Ephesians 4:15, we must speak the truth in love, as Sande points out:

> When you need to show others their faults, do not talk down to them as though you are faultless and they are inferior to you. Instead, talk with them as though you are standing side by side at the foot of the cross. Acknowledge your present, ongoing need for the Savior. Admit ways that you have wrestled with the same or other sins or weaknesses, and give hope by describing how God has forgiven you and is currently working to help you change.... When people sense this kind of humility and common bond, they will be less inclined to react to correction with pride and defensiveness.[11]

11. Ibid.

Coming to a brother or sister in Christ as their friend will also enable you to relax and not feel awkward at the beginning of the conversation. This is especially true for Christian bosses who oversee other Christians. Jesus's approach to others is what has been called "power under control." In other words, Jesus is in a position to overpower others, but because he is holy, never misuses that power to lord it over his enemies or his friends. The Son of God approaches others humbly. How much more are we, as redeemed sinners, required to do the same?

This is a practical outworking of the Golden Rule of our Lord in the Sermon on the Mount: "So whatever you wish that others would do for you, do also for them, for this is the Law and the Prophets" (Matt. 7:12). Applied to our speech, the Lord here obligates his followers to speak to others as they would want to be spoken to by others. Would you want others to tear into you, assuming the worst motives? Would you want others to assume you are guilty of some offense without ever giving you the opportunity to speak and adjudicate yourself? Would you want to be called names or be the subject of sarcastic insults? Then we must avoid talking to others in ways that denigrate them. In saying "for this is the Law and the Prophets," Jesus is saying that treating others with kindness, justice, and equity is fulfilling the Law's demands to love God and love your neighbor. We must communicate accordingly.

## 10. REMEMBER YOU'RE TALKING TO SOMEONE PRECIOUS TO CHRIST, AND YOU'RE ALWAYS DIALOGUING CORAM DEO.

If you're talking to a Christian, then you're talking with a person for whom the Lord shed his blood; a person valuable to him (1 Cor. 8:11; Rom. 14:15). John Crotts writes, "How precious is the weakest Christian in the body of Christ? What does Jesus think about their value? These weak Christians are as valuable as the blood of the Lord Jesus Christ."[12]

Also, remember what Christ admonished us to do in the Sermon on the Mount: treat others the way you want to be treated. Do you want to be demeaned? Do you want to be made to feel small? Or do you want to be treated with dignity, as a person made in God's image?

---

12. Crotts, *Graciousness*, location 1017.

Remember, too, that an omnipresent, omniscient God is monitoring your mouth, and he is concerned about the details. This should help us to filter out harsh, critical language. Crotts makes a sobering point: "[If] you knew that God was listening to every word that you were saying and was instantaneously aware of the slightest inflections of your voice, and that He would hold you accountable according to the highest standards of his holiness, would you not speak to others with the utmost care?"[13]

We must also realize that are times when it is simply impossible to be at peace with another person. Paul anticipates this in Romans 12:18, but his words are instructive as to our manner of treating our opponents even when they won't be reconciled to us: "If it is possible, as much as depends on you, live peaceably with all men." We must do all we can to promote peace in our bearing and in our dialogue. But after we've done all we can and things remain volatile, we must prayerfully leave the results in God's hands and remember that Christ loved his enemies. And he has called us to do the same.

Richard Wurmbrand, a Lutheran pastor in Romania, spent more than 12 years in prison at the hands of atheistic Communist leaders from the late 1940s until 1964. He was repeatedly beaten and starved in various squalid prison camps where he was kept near Bucharest. He was interrogated dozens of times and subjected to brainwashing along with all the other Romanian pastors who had resisted the godless doctrines of Communism. Yet in all the interrogations, even when they turned violent, he maintained the loving demeanor and tone of Christ, which led to the conversion of numerous interrogators and caused many others to be friendlier toward him, astonished that he could love those who hated him so. "For Richard . . . love became more powerful than violence, for it could subdue the heart of even the most ruthless interrogator."[14] Is this not reminiscent of the way Christ handled those who nailed him to the cross? Even on that darkest of days, as our Savior bled and died for us, he prayed for his murderers, "Father, forgive them, for they know not what they do" (Luke 23:34). Christ's love in the face of the harshest treatment should color both our words and also our tone in every conflicted conversation.

13. Ibid.
14. Wurmbrand, *Tortured for Christ*, Kindle edition, location 3838.

## BOTTOM LINE

In navigating minefield conversations, we want neither to underreact nor overreact. To underreact may mean we are flirting with compromise, fleeing a necessary but difficult confrontation, or we're not treating the issues being discussed with the seriousness they deserve. To overreact may lead to relational fractures, an outbreak of sinful anger, or worse. One is a sin of omission, the other is a sin of commission. One response is too passive, the other too aggressive. Both are sinful and lead us into further sin. As followers of Christ, called to do all things to the glory of God (1 Cor. 10:31), we must guard against both extremes. We must ask the Lord to give us a healthy, biblical balance in the way we talk to others, and seek his help to deal with difficult conversations in a Christ-like manner, full of both grace and truth.

## MEMORY VERSE

*A soft answer turns away wrath, but a harsh word stirs up anger.* (Prov. 15:1)

## QUESTIONS FOR GROUP DISCUSSION

1. Why do we tend to notice the tone of a conversation when it's not normal? What types of tone most quickly get our attention?
2. Some have said the Bible doesn't address tone. How does Scripture demonstrate that God not only wants us to weigh our words, but also to pay attention to *how* we say things?
3. Why does the author tie tone to humility? Why is the Bible so concerned that God's people develop humility?
4. How would humility help a difficult conversation with another person on theology, politics, social issues, or family dynamics? What words could you insert to help the conversation remain civil?
5. Consider practicing these difficult conversations with another believer in your church or small group. Identify a difficult topic and work through it in accordance with the principles given in this chapter for difficult conversation. It could be an issue you're working through as a parent, a son or daughter, in the church or at work. Some ideas: You're a political conservative talking to your daughter, who has just told you she's pro-abortion and pro-same-sex marriage. Or what would you say to your child whom you catechized and raised in church if they informed

you they were gay? How could you speak the truth in love as a follower of Jesus, who is full of grace and truth? (John 1:14)

6. How can navigating certain conversations be like trying to survive a trek across a minefield?

7. How should you prepare yourself spiritually to enter into a minefield conversation? What three questions might Roger Nicole have us ask?

8. How much should we assume entering into a difficult conversation? Are we really able to know the other person's motives with perfect accuracy? What does Matthew 7:1–5 say about that, and why is that such an important passage for us all?

9. Why are emotions so dangerous, and how should we handle them if we know we're entering a hard dialogue?

10. How can your body language hinder clear, accurate communication?

11. What does Paul's encounter with Agrippa in Acts 26:3 demonstrate that can help our talk?

12. What are clarity words, and why are they absolutely vital for dialogue that is long on light and short on heat?

13. Read Matthew 18:21–35, the parable of the unforgiving servant. Discuss the main lesson from Jesus. How is it related to our interactions with others? What does it have to do with humility and our overall bearing as Christians in every setting?

14. How could posturing yourself as a friend and not an enemy change the tenor of a dialogue in which you are confronting another believer? What about confronting one of your children or an intimate friend?

## FOR FURTHER READING AND STUDY

- *The Peacemaker: A Biblical Guide to Resolving Personal Conflict* (Baker, 2004) by Ken Sande
- *Graciousness: Tempering Truth with Love* (Reformation Heritage, 2018) by John Crotts
- *I Beg to Differ: Navigating Difficult Conversations with Truth and Love* (IVP, 2014) by Tim Muehlhoff
- *Speaking the Truth in Love: The Life & Legacy of Roger Nicole* (Solid Ground Christian Books, 2006) by David W. Bailey. I especially commend Nicole's widely circulated essay, which is included as Appendix 1, "How to Deal with Those Who Differ from Us." That essay is readily available online.
- *Gospel-Powered Humility* (P&R, 2011) by William P. Farley

CHAPTER 6

# TALKING WITH
# OUR THUMBS

*"If anyone thinks he is religious without controlling his thumb, his religion is useless and he deceives himself." —Matt Smethurst on James 1:26 for a smartphone age*

*Turn my eyes from looking at worthless things; and give me life in your ways.*
(Ps. 119:37)

The National Weather Service has a rarely used designation for situations when long-track, strong, and violent tornadoes or extreme severe thunderstorms are possible on a given day: Particularly Dangerous Situation (PDS). To my recollection, I've only heard the PDS declared three or four times in the past decade or so, and on each occasion, there was a pretty serious tornado outbreak in the Midwest and Deep South.

I want to issue a PDS warning for a particular form of communication that's relatively new, but is wildly popular: social media. Unless you've been left alone on a deserted island for the past decade or so, you know I'm talking about platforms such as Facebook, Twitter, and Instagram. For our hearts, they represent a PDS when it comes to the warnings of Scripture aimed at how Christians are expected to use their words. For example, how many of us post things on Facebook that make us look bad? Is our life really as rich, joyful, and fulfilling as we let on? Do we really spend most of our time at the beach or enjoying a robust laugh with our well-behaved, high-functioning children? Is that telling the whole truth about ourselves?

Maybe it's because I'm a little old school, I'm not sure (I grew up dialing a phone and listening to music on cassette tapes), but I'll admit that I'm scared to death of social media. Because of my work for The Gospel Coalition, which daily leverages social media to share gospel-centered content to the masses, I'm in the realm of social media often. I'm grateful for the way TGC and similar ministries employ social media. My wife and I have a joint Facebook account, and I use Twitter almost exclusively to follow other Christians, to get instant updates on news, and to follow baseball and college football.

But I rarely tweet. Why? There is nothing intrinsically wrong about using Facebook or Twitter. To use or not to use is a preference. But for me, it comes down to three things. One, I prefer to read and write books and articles. Much of my adult life has been spent doing that work. Second, I have precious time left over once I've served my callings as a husband, father, pastor, editor/writer, adjunct professor, and amateur golfer. OK, there's not much room for golf these days, but all the other stuff gives me a fulfilling but crazy life. Social media is designed to be addictive, and right now, an addiction will make a mess of those things. But the third reason may be the most important: I don't trust myself or the medium. I'm a sinner who doesn't always use words well, has a history of struggles with anger, and tends toward holding strong convictions. Think about Justine Sacco's life-exploding tweet. The thought of a long thread of nasty responses following an ill-advised comment by me on Twitter almost gives me hives. It's not that I mind polemics or giving my opinion; it's that I've read Proverbs 10:19: "When words are many, sin is not lacking." I'll have enough sinful words to give an account for on that day; being hyperactive on Twitter is not worth having to give more. Plus, I'm a pastor. I'd rather my congregation know what I think about a given issue because they've talked to me about it and not from Twitter debates in which I've been involved.

All the aforementioned warnings and wisdom principles apply to social media, but in a somewhat limited fashion—which is why social media is itself limited and poses so many dangers as a means of relationship building and communication. Here are my concerns, and why I think we need to issue a PDS and take special care with our words when it comes to communicating anywhere on the internet.

## 1. THE HOT TAKE IS NOT ALWAYS THE WISE TAKE.

And perhaps it would be more accurate, and, in keeping with a major theme of this book, more charitable to say the hot take is *almost never* the humble, wise take. I have only circumstantial evidence (but lots of it) to support that statement. Breaking news is necessary for newspapers and magazines—the thing for which I use Twitter the most. But it's not always necessary for us, especially if we're responding to controversy. Thoughts need time to mature, words need time to be carefully crafted, ideas and views need careful study and close scrutiny. All this requires patience—the opposite of the hot take.

How often do we overreact to something that stirs our emotions, and by the next day we either regret how we responded or give thanks we did not? For me, that's about nine out of 10 times. "Let us be slow to speak and quick to listen" (James 1:19). Or, as the proverb variously attributed puts it, "Better to remain silent and be thought a fool than to open your mouth and remove all doubt."

## 2. EDITORS EXIST FOR A (GOOD) REASON.

I know that sounds self-serving, since I've long made part of my living as a copy repairman. And, granted, Solomon didn't have editors in mind when he wrote Proverbs, but I think the principle in Proverbs 11:14 applies: "Where there is no guidance, a people falls, but in an abundance of counselors there is safety." Beware of social media users who are uncomfortable with others reading and weighing in on or revising their posts prior to publication. Especially beware of those who style themselves as "discernment" bloggers. Usually, it only takes a quick glance on any given day to learn there's no discernment (and no editors/outside readers). They exist because the internet is a vast libertarian continent. The U.S. Constitution guarantees free speech, but the Bible puts wise guard rails on how the people of God are to speak freely.

Unless we seek it out, and I'm guessing few of us do, given the informal nature of social media banter, there's no accountability for what we say to others on Twitter or Facebook. The same is true for blogs. Usually, there's no referee. One of the things that makes written communication superior when it appears in books (non-self-published), newspapers, or magazines is that articles and even opinion columns have usually been through several channels of rather rigorous editing and fact- and source-checking. After nearly three decades as a journalist and editor, this is probably the number one reason why I'm hesitant to use Twitter or Facebook. As a writer, I need an editor. As a sinner, I need accountability.

Many have told me they find blogging and social media attractive precisely because they are unfettered by gatekeepers or editors, and I understand that appeal on one level. But I as told one armchair pundit who was a student in my church history class, writers who write well and think well tend to get hired as writers, regardless of their perspective on the theological/political/social spectrum.

### 3. WRITTEN WORDS HAVE A LONGER SHELF LIFE THAN SPOKEN WORDS.

This is true for the simple reason that written words are always and forever "out there."

A pastor friend once sent out an abrupt and ill-advised tweet in response to a snarky message aimed at one of his friends. After rethinking his words for five minutes, he deleted the tweet. However, the original tweeter, if that's a word, had taken note and saved it. A phone call and a series of long talks was needed to reconcile them.

Another friend who oversaw his company's social media accounts inadvertently tweeted out some sensitive information at his job. Though he caught his honest mistake and deleted it two minutes after it went out, a number of media members took note and wrote a news story on the topic he had tweeted. My friend was fired.

Of course, time and space would fail me were I to begin to speak about social-media mobs and their dirty work. Suffice it to say, the mob as we traditionally think of it has nothing on them in bullying a dissenting opinion or sullying a good reputation.

## 4. RESPONSES ON SOCIAL MEDIA ARE UNABLE TO ACCURATELY DEPICT THE EMOTIONAL STATE OF THE RESPONDER.

Yes, I know, that's what emoji are for—smiley faces, winky faces, angry faces. And, of course, we have the comments section for online articles and posts. But what we don't have is our tone of voice, our body language, frowns, smiles, laughter, playful sarcasm, and other emotions that make the conversation a three-dimensional event. The comments section falls prey to the same dangers as the article, blog, post, or tweet itself. How many of us would say most comments and commenters succeed in offering wisdom and graciously move the discussion down the road?

Written communication can be impersonal—we are separated by space and even time from the reader—and one-dimensional, so we must take every precaution to make certain our messages are heard in the spirit in which they're offered. One of my newspaper colleagues captured this well in answering a man who called our office to complain about his editorial. "I'm a little offended," he said, to which my friend replied, "Oh, I'm sorry, I meant to offend you a lot!"

## 5. ONLINE COMMUNICATION IS OFTEN ANONYMOUS AND LACKING ACCOUNTABILITY.

I'm convinced people say things to others on Facebook or Twitter they'd never say to their face. It takes courage to say something hard to another person while in their presence. It takes no courage at all to type an insult and hit "post," because we're completely removed from that person and have no idea what effect it will have on them or even their good name. Spatial distance allows for this reality. No doubt, you'd be far more careful with your rhetoric, and you might even wind up being kind, if you had to sit across the table to address that person. It's why if I must have a difficult conversation with one of my church members and cannot meet with them, I'll have a conversation with them on the phone or by Skype or FaceTime. Those media can achieve a more similar "proximity" effect to the face-to-face conversation.

## 6. SOCIAL MEDIA ATTRACTS AND REWARDS THE RHETORICAL AGENT PROVOCATEUR.

Social media tends to attract and reward the extremes. How can you gain 500 likes or 10,000 followers? Probably not by posting Bible verses or Puritan quotes. You gain a following by provocation, and extreme opinions tend to provoke likes (or anger emojis) or gain followers. Members of the fringe within every group tend to shout the loudest, gain the most attention, tend to be the proverbial squeaky wheel.

Social media plays well for extremists and their opinions because they gain the most hearers and make the most enemies. It's just not the place for serious, fruitful debate and discussion of complex issues that demand careful nuance. Social media also manipulates our desire for approval. The more followers and commenters support our cause and pat us on the back, the less likely we are to reflect critically or receive correction about what we've said. We're more likely to double down because we want the chorus of approval to gain more and louder voices.

In a Christian context, I'd say the more mature a believer is, the less likely he or she is to be a provocateur. With this in mind, my friend Matt Smethurst's words on Twitter ought to be kept in mind: "An immature Christian is hard to please and easy to offend." Why do mature Christians spend so much time on social media? I can't give an objective answer to that question, but it's worth pondering, and it's something I've asked mainly about myself in thinking how I should regulate my time on the internet.

## 7. THE WHOLE WORLD IS NOT ON TWITTER.

There are 7 billion people in the world, but only 126 million daily users on Twitter. Those 25 angry responses to your tweet on social justice, or free will theology, or Democrat/Republican shenanigans are really insignificant, in spite of what you may think. Getting, say, 300 comments on Twitter or 400 likes on Facebook does not mean that a great cloud of witnesses has gathered around you or your pet issue. While you're debating the number of angels that can dance on a pinhead or whether Adam had a belly button, most of us are working, spending time with family, friends, or church members.

We're at the golf course, ballpark, hiking in the mountains, or lounging at the beach.

As one of the many crotchety newspaper editors I worked alongside during my journalism career once said, "Nobody really cares about what you've got to say." I don't intend for that statement to sound contrary to the sort of tone I've sought to establish in this book. Yet as a bald, unemotional statement it's true. Two of the ugliest theological debates I've witnessed on Twitter the past few years involved the Trinity and social justice. Those debates were intense for a few of us, but only a few of us. We must keep that in mind. My congregation hardly noticed either debate, and I feel certain the good people at my church are fairly typical.

## CAN WE USE IT FRUITFULLY?

I believe Christians and Christian leaders can use social media for good purposes. It's great for recommending good books and sharing Bible passages. It makes it easy to get in touch with other people.

One of my mentors, who has been in ministry for more than 50 years, regularly writes letters to those with whom he has fairly serious theological differences. I've seen many of his letters and have spoken to those to whom he's written. Though they continue to disagree—even profoundly in some cases—to a person they have all remarked about how congenial and fruitful the debates have been. That approach helps to avoid the hit-and-run nature of Twitter.

Christians should use social media with great care and resist the urge to spend so much time on social media or to mistakenly think that conversations there fully reflect the real world or the majority of people in their local church.

## REMEMBER: EVERY IDLE WORD

Back in chapter 2, we examined one of the most frightening sentences to fall from the lips of Jesus: "I tell you, on the day of judgment people will give account for every careless word they speak, for by your words you will be justified, and by your words you will be condemned" (Matt. 12:37–37).

When we read these words from Jesus, we tend to think only of words that come from our mouths. But it seems safe to assume that our Lord would also say that we'll give an account for every careless word we write, tweet, text, or email, so let's double down with how we love our neighbors in every medium of electronic and printed communication. It's certainly not a sin to use social media, provided we use them with care. But let's think and pray before we type and hit send, lest we damage our relationship with our neighbor and our Lord. It is a particularly dangerous situation. We need to be slow to speak and slow to type and quick to listen.

It may seem odd in a book on talk, but let's finish our conversation with a discussion about our Christian duty to listen.

## MEMORY VERSE

*I will not set before my eyes any worthless thing.* (Ps. 101:3a)

## QUESTIONS FOR GROUP DISCUSSION

1. How many hours per day do you spend on social media? How might you better use your time? If your screen time is excessive, what kind of plan might you formulate to cut down on it?
2. How do you think about the words you use on Facebook, Twitter, or other online platforms? How do the principles in the previous chapters of this book apply to your use of words online?
3. What are some ways you might use social media for redemptive purposes? Discuss how the internet has helped you as a follower of Christ.

## FOR FURTHER READING
## AND STUDY

- *12 Ways Your Phone Is Changing You* (Crossway, 2017) by Tony Reinke
- *The Tech-Wise Family: Everyday Steps for Putting Technology in Its Proper Place* (Baker, 2017) by Andy Crouch

CHAPTER 7

# TWO EARS,
# ONE MOUTH

*Know this, my beloved brothers: let every person be quick to hear, slow to speak, slow to anger. (James 1:19)*

*It is a great thing to have an open ear. Some are very slow to hear, especially to hear the Word of God, and the voice of God speaking in that Word. Oh, to have our ears unstopped, that we may hear every syllable of truth gladly, cheerfully, retentively! God grant us that swiftness of hearing...For, sometimes, when men are very quick to speak, they are also very quick in other respects as well; and volubility may be accompanied by a tendency to heat or passion. —C. H. Spurgeon from a sermon on James 1:19*

My children aren't good listeners; I suspect they inherited that particular deficiency from their dad. One of my favorite high school teachers used to tell me, "Robinson, God gave you two ears and one mouth for a reason. That tell you anything?" To no one's surprise, the thing that got me in trouble consistently throughout my years in school was my mouth. It's been the same

with my kids. The notes we've received from teachers over the years expressing concerns about their behavior all related to talking. And I've used that
line—two ears, one mouth—many times with my two sons and two daughters, yet they still struggle to hear their mom and me when we're telling
them something important.

Today, I'm a pastor, so I've had to work hard at listening, I mean, really
listening so I can get all the information right, and listening so I can empathize or respond properly. I suspect many of us—even those of us who get
paid to listen—are not as good at listening as we might think we are, since
we tend to think more highly of ourselves than we ought. From my experiences and observations, there are four subtle ways we feign listening to
others—perhaps without even realizing it—while not really doing so:

1.  *Impatient listening.* This is when I'm in a conversation, and I wait for
    you to pause for a nanosecond so I can inject my point or respond to
    yours. We're listening only to respond, often gaining only bits and pieces
    of information.

2.  *Better opportunity listening.* The most impolite form of pretend listening,
    this happens when we're in a room with a larger group of people, and
    we're in conversation. We're sort of listening, nodding, and respond-
    ing with one word such as, "Yes" or "Really?" or "Great!" But our eyes
    are fixed over the shoulder of the other person. We're scanning for a
    better conversation or perhaps a way of escape. Bottom line: we're not
    really listening.

3.  *Debate listening.* This is similar but slightly different than impatient lis-
    tening. This is when we're in a conversation with someone with whom
    we disagree. In this situation, we're merely gleaning key facts so we can
    jump in and refute their arguments. When we listen this way, we tend to
    miss what the other person is really saying.

4.  *Polite, but not listening.* My wife says I'm an expert at this type of non-lis-
    tening, and I fear she's correct. It may be that pastors particularly strug-
    gle with this form of non-listening. This type of listener never learns
    your name or never remembers you despite having met you multiple
    times. There is a well-known Southern Baptist pastor who has talked
    with me repeatedly over the years. We've had lengthy conversations, we
    grew up in virtually the same place, and he's met my family several times.
    Yet a common encounter with him goes something like this (He never
    lacks confidence that he knows my name): "Hey, Jim, it's great to see

you. How's your sweet wife, Linda?" Of course you know my first name, because it's printed on the cover of this book, and my wife's name is Lisa. Not Linda, but close. He once asked how "Leslie" was doing. I really enjoy talking to this man, but I would feel better about our conversations if he'd remember our names. I get the feeling he's not really listening.

Does any of this sound familiar? I'm guilty of such non-listening far more than I should be—especially as a pastor. Through the first five chapters, I've sought to help us become better and more Christlike talkers, but no book on talk would be complete without a good discussion of how we can better be on the receiving end of words. After all, none of us should merely talk and talk and talk. If most of us use 20,000 words per day, I've met prodigious talkers who surely bump the word count up well beyond 50,000. You likely know all too well how draining those people can be. I don't want to be that person, for it's surely not counting the other person better than ourselves, not loving our neighbor well when we vomit words and sentences endlessly as if we're attempting a Senate filibuster.

More importantly, Scripture puts an important accent on listening—it depicts the wise person as the hearing person. The Bible also has some unvarnished words for those who prattle on ceaselessly and seem to have little time for hearing the words and opinions of others.

A fool takes no pleasure in understanding, but only in expressing his opinion. (Prov. 18:2)

If one gives an answer before he hears, it is his folly and shame. (Prov. 18:13)

Do you see a man who is hasty in his words? There is more hope for a fool than for him. (Prov. 29:20)

Know this, my beloved brothers: let every person be quick to hear, slow to speak, slow to anger. (James 1:19)

The fool doesn't take time to listen, and he doesn't take time to ponder what the other person has said. One wonders if perhaps this was the malady that infected Job's three friends Eliphaz, Bildad, and Zophar. If ever there were a hall of fame for poor listeners, these three might be the most highly decorated inductees.

We may listen, but we don't listen well. Remember the whisper game you played in middle school? Someone whispered a fact into one person's ear, and they in turn did the same to the person next to them. This continued through a long line until the person at the end of the chain reported on what was said. Most of the time it was completely different from what the first person whispered to the second.

Deepak Reju argues that several things lead to poor listening: impatience, tiredness (This affects how we listen to sermons, too), zoning out, and interrupting others: "Your thought is so pressing—and your tongue is loose—that you blurt things out before the other person is even done speaking."[1]

How can we follow James's admonition to be slow to speak but also quick to listen? As followers of Christ, listening to gain accurate information, to know how to help or pray for another person, to learn how we can empathize or help another believer is an important part of living out the Bible's "one another" commands within the body of Christ. Sometimes we need to listen well before we're able to speak wisely into a given situation. I'm convinced the more prone we are to talking, the more we will need to prayerfully develop our skill in listening well.

## HOW CAN WE BE QUICK TO LISTEN?

In the opening chapter, I argued that words are vital because God has spoken to us through words and phrases and clauses. But when we are reading and meditating on his Word, what are we really doing? We're hearing from him. We're hearers of the Word of God. When we listen to sermons we are hearers of the Word of God. Yes, God wants talkers, but more than that, as David Powlison argues, he wants listeners.[2] He wants people who not only listen, but who do so with their whole heart. Why? Because God wants to tell us about himself—and we grow by listening, not by talking (thus, one mouth, two ears).

---

1.    Deepak Reju, "Listen Up! Practical Help for Lousy Listeners," The Gospel Coalition, July 18, 2019, https://www.thegospelcoalition.org/article/listen-up-help-lousy-listeners. Accessed July 24, 2019.
2.    David Powlison, *Speaking the Truth in Love: Counsel in Community* (Greensboro, NC: New Growth Press, 2005), 83.

For more than two decades, I worked as a newspaper journalist, and my work required that I interview people regularly. I was privileged to interview people from every walk of life from PGA golfers, Major League Baseball players, and college football players to a Top Gun pilot, a convicted murderer on death row, a witch, an Army general, a paramilitary leader, and dozens of "everyday" people. The people and their stories were the reason I enjoyed my years in journalism. I had to learn to listen to gain accurate information. I needed to ask good follow-up questions. Here are a few tips on how to become a better listener.

1. *Listen before you answer.* You want to hear what the other person is saying. Don't be like Job's friends, who apparently listened selectively. Listen well so you will be able to respond with laser-focused words of life. This will help us not to jump to rash conclusions if we're involved in conflict or have been sought out by another believer for counsel. Without what Ken Sande calls "waiting," you will often fail to understand the root cause of a conflict and then make things worse by reacting inappropriately.[3] It is critical to learn the lesson of Proverbs 18:13: "If one gives an answer before he hears, it is his folly and shame."

2. *Don't go numb and bug out.* My tendency, whether I was doing an interview for an article or performing a pastoral counseling session, is to let a mental fog envelop me and stop listening, especially when listening to an incessant talker. As Sande points out, the human mind can think at least four times faster than a person can talk, so our minds tend to get bored and look for something more to do like rehearsing our responses, which short-circuits good listening.

3. *Maintain regular eye contact.* Eliminate distractions. Turn off your phone or the television or close the door if there is noise outside. Lean forward, which shows interest, and try to use soft facial expressions. A bored or angry look can shut down the other person. Nod your head or occasionally and use verbal signals that indicate you're still listening and following them.

4. *Don't get irritated, especially if they are saying things you don't like.* If you're irritated, don't give it away through facial expressions. God commands that we be patient with one another because he is patient with us.

---

3. Sande, *The Peacemaker*, 165.

5.  *Don't let them chase rabbits.* Ask well-placed questions to put some guard-rails on the discussion.

6.  *Seek clarification.* Ask questions like, "Have I understood you accurately?" and then recount what you've understood them to say. This way, you can clear up misunderstandings, partial understandings, and glean further information.

7.  *Don't let sinful talk repel you.* Once I was in a counseling session when the counselee (a non-Christian man seeking to be reconciled to his Christian wife) peppered his talk with F-bombs. I wasn't necessarily surprised or offended by his use of profanity (after all, I grew up around baseball players and building contractors), but I was distracted and thrown off my counseling game. As David Powlison points out, "You will almost invariably hear sins in the process (of listening). You'll hear bitterness, gossip, self-pity, false belief, rationalization, obsession, evasion, fabrication—the thousand tongues of foolish and empty talk."[4]

8.  *Agree with them as much as possible.* This is a valuable tactic that Ken Sande recommends, one I've tried to use, particularly when the conversation is unpleasant or involves conflict. For example, you could say, "I can understand why you would be upset that we've made changes in the church music program," or "You are correct, I don't have as much experience in this area as I'd like, and you do know much more about it than I do."[5] Agreeing, Sande writes, "doesn't mean you abandon your beliefs, but rather that you acknowledge what you know is true before addressing points of disagreement. Agreeing with the person who is speaking will often encourage him or her to talk more openly and avoid unnecessary repetition. Agreeing is especially important when you have been in the wrong.... [It] can make the difference between an argument and a meaningful dialogue."[6] Such admissions also display a measure of humility that can encourage others to talk with you and use a more gracious tone, especially if they are criticizing you—a kind of talk we all find especially difficult to hear.

9.  *Listen to hear them, not to correct, judge, or coach them.* Whether you are a pastor or layperson, sometimes you just need to be with a hurting person and furnish them with a listening, sympathetic, or even empathetic, ear.

---

4.  Powlison, *Speaking the Truth in Love*, 85.
5.  Sande, *The Peacemaker*, 168.
6.  Ibid.

About two years into my first full-time pastorate, a family in our church lost their infant grandson to crib death on the first night they kept him. Naturally, they were broken beyond words. My wife and I spent much of the next morning with them, and all I really did was pray with them when we first arrived and when we left—it was a Sunday morning, and I had to preach for our congregation. I wasn't certain I had done anything to soothe their suffering other than to weep with them and hear their hurt. Several weeks later they met with me and commended me for how I had ministered to them just by being there. "You've taught us about the sovereignty of God and how life in a fallen world is full of pain, and you've taught us about Christ's suffering for us," the grandmother said through tears. "You didn't need to do that again, and you didn't. You and Lisa were just there with us, hurting alongside us, and we were comforted by your presence and your prayers." As I try to teach my pastoral interns, sometimes you just need to be with them and say it best by saying nothing at all. When Jesus raised Lazarus from the dead, he didn't tell Mary to stop crying, or that he was going to fix everything in a few minutes—even though he was going to raise him from the dead. He wept with her.

## SHOULD I HAVE LISTENED MORE?

My father was a godly, wise man. He fought in World War II and made three jumps in combat, won a Purple Heart and other medals for bravery in war. He was humble and slow to speak. People in our church and in our community listened to him. Dad died in 1991 when I was a senior in college. But one of the things I can still hear him saying to this day if I close my eyes is this: "Jeff, you will almost never regret having said nothing. It's hard to sin verbally with your mouth closed." That's great advice. It's Proverbs, James, Paul, and Jesus applied.

Another friend put the same truth differently. He said, "I wonder if, when we come to the end of our lives, we'll wish we'd said more or we'll wish we'd said less, especially to those closest to us like our wives and kids."

Sure, there's a time to speak, but there's also a time to listen. Solomon said as much in Ecclesiastes 3. There are times we need to stand up for the truth or speak out against injustice, and to not speak would spell cowardice. But, over the span of our lives—50, 60, 70, even 80 or 90 years—those moments are relatively rare. But how often will we wish we would've listened instead of talked? Maybe we should've listened more to our sons and daughters instead of lecturing them so much. I think James answers that question: Let us be slow to speak and quick to listen. Two ears, one mouth.

## MEMORY VERSE

*The one who states his case first seems right, until the other comes and examines him.* (Prov. 18:17)

## QUESTIONS FOR GROUP DISCUSSION

1. What are some forms of non-listening that we often disguise as listening? Which one of these do you tend toward?
2. How does the Bible connect wisdom with listening?
3. Were Job's friends really listening to their friend's concerns? Why or why not?
4. Discuss the nine tips for how we can be quick to listen. How can you put these to work within your closest relationships? How can you put these to work in your church?
5. When you come to the end of your life, do you think you'll be more likely to wish you'd talked more or listened more? To your kids? Your spouse? Your friends? Your church leaders?

## FOR FURTHER READING AND STUDY

- *Speaking the Truth in Love: Counsel in Community* (New Growth Press, 2005) by David Powlison
- *Instruments in the Redeemer's Hands: People in Need of Change Helping People in Need of Change* (P&R, 2002) by Paul David Tripp

# HEARTS AND TONGUES SET FREE

Jesus's words in Matthew 12:36–37 are profoundly sobering: "I tell you, on the day of judgment people will give account for every careless word they speak, for by your words you will be justified, and by your words you will be condemned." Think about it: every sinful word multiplied by 20,000 opportunities every single day. And the words? They tell what's really in your heart. Is your heart full of love, joy, peace, patience, kindness, goodness, faithfulness, and self-control? The words that come from your mouth answer that question with brutal honesty.

What shape would our talk take if we lived daily with that truth on the front of our minds? Would we still criticize others on social media? Would we whisper to our co-workers about those things we don't like about our boss or our job? Would we speak slanderously about our political leaders?

What might dialogue within our families look like? Would we call our teenage son a quitter because he doesn't want to play soccer anymore? Would we call our daughter lazy when she brings home a B in history? Would we call our parents clueless when they didn't totally embrace our choice of music? How would we talk to our spouse when they don't please us? If we spoke graciously and carefully, would we avoid most of the squabbles that tend to interrupt the harmony in our homes?

What about our churches? If we weighed every single word, surely the elders would get along well. If we did that, then Paul would've likely avoided admonishing Euodia and Syntyche to "agree in the Lord" (Phil. 4:2). Apparently those ladies were scuffling with one another; no doubt sinful words were exchanged between them. What would pastors say about their members, and what would members say about the shepherds whom God has raised up to lead them?

If we took Jesus's words with the seriousness our Savior intended, every relationship and sphere in our lives would be affected for good—it would give us a taste of heaven. Imagine a world without slander, gossip, bitterness, cursing, sinful criticism, boasting, grumbling, name-calling, and mean-spirited sarcasm. It would look like heaven.

This book has focused mainly with how we misuse words and how God's grace transforms our talk so our communication is joyful and beautiful and honoring to the one who made our tongues and gave us voices to speak. The same Savior who warned us that words would justify or condemn on the last day also said, "I am the resurrection and the life. Whoever believes in me, though he die, yet shall he live" (John 11:25).

No longer are our hearts and tongues enslaved to sin and death. Think of all the ways the transformed tongue now works to the glory of God. We give thanks to him for saving us and providing for us. We proclaim his name through preaching, teaching, and evangelism. We worship him privately and corporately in our churches, homes, and workplaces. We fill our heart and mind with his Word so that our lips bubble over with praise.

Think of the glorious hymns that Jesus's followers have written and now sing with beautiful words that celebrate his unfathomable love for sinners.

"Peace on earth and mercy mild, God and sinner reconciled."

"Oh the bliss of this glorious thought: my sin, not in part, but the whole is nailed to the cross and I bear it no more.... Praise the Lord, it is well with my soul!"

"Long my imprisoned spirit lay, fast bound by sin and nature's night. Thine eye diffused a quickening ray, I woke, the dungeon flamed with light; my chains fell off, my heart was free, I rose, went forth, and followed thee."

"Amazing grace, how sweet the sound, that saved a wretch like me; I once was lost, but now I'm found; t'was blind, but now I see."

"See, from his head, his hands, his feet, sorrow and love flow mingled down; Did e'er such love and sorrow meet, or thorns compose so rich a crown?"

"There is a fountain, filled with blood, drawn from Emmanuel's veins; and sinners plunged beneath that flood lose all their guilty stains."

"No guilt in life, no fear in death; This is the power of Christ in me."

"Our sins, they are many, his mercy is more."

"And we are raised in him; death is dead, love has won, Christ has conquered."

Though the redeemed wrestle with indwelling sin, and our talk is by no means perfect, still the Holy Spirit and not the serpent now rides the stallion in our mouths.

Think of the prayers and praise that now comes from our lips.

"Bless the LORD, O my soul, and all that is within me, bless his holy name!"

"Not to us, O LORD, not to us, but to your name give glory, for the sake of your steadfast love and faithfulness!"

"Our Father in heaven, hallowed be thy name."

"Oh, the depth of the riches and wisdom and knowledge of God! How unsearchable are his judgments and how inscrutable his ways!"

"Now to him who is able to keep you from stumbling and to present you blameless before the presence of his glory with great joy, to the only God, our Savior, through Jesus Christ our Lord, be glory, majesty, dominion, and authority, before all time and now and forever. Amen."

May it please our great and sovereign God, the God of peace, who brought again from the dead our Lord Jesus, the great shepherd of the sheep, by the blood of the eternal covenant, to equip us, especially our tongues, with everything good that we may do his will, talking and singing and rejoicing and worshiping and listening and writing and communicating always, in every platform and setting, such that our words and our relationships are pleasing in his sight.

# MEMORY VERSES ON TALK

EXODUS 20:7
You shall not take the name of the LORD your God in vain, for the Lord will not hold him guiltless who takes his name in vain.

PSALM 15:1–3
O LORD, who shall sojourn in your tent? Who shall dwell on our holy hill? He who walks blamelessly and does what is right and speaks truth in his heart; who does not slander with his tongue and does no evil to his neighbor, nor takes up a reproach against his friend;

PSALM 141:3
Set a guard, O LORD, over my mouth;
keep watch over the door of my lips!

PROVERBS 10:11
The mouth of the righteous is a fountain of life, but the mouth of the wicked conceives violence.

PROVERBS 10:14

The wise lay up knowledge, but the mouth of a fool brings ruin near.

PROVERBS 10:18

The one who conceals hatred has lying lips, and whoever utters slander is a fool.

PROVERBS 10:19

When words are many, transgression is not lacking, but whoever restrains his lips is prudent.

PROVERBS 10:20–21

The tongue of righteous is choice silver; the heart of the wicked is of little worth. The lips of the righteous feed many. But fools die for lack of sense.

PROVERBS 10:31–32

The mouth of the righteous brings forth wisdom, but the perverse tongue will be cut off. The lips of the righteous know what is acceptable, but the mouth of the wicked, what is perverse.

PROVERBS 11:12

Whoever belittles his neighbor lacks sense, but a man of understanding remains silent.

PROVERBS 11:13

Whoever goes about slandering reveals secrets, but he who is trustworthy in spirit keeps a thing covered.

PROVERBS 12:18

There is one whose rash words are like sword thrusts, but the tongue of the wise brings healing.

PROVERBS 13:3

Whoever guards his mouth preserves his life; he who opens wise his lips comes to ruin.

PROVERBS 15:1–2

A soft answer turns away wrath, but a harsh word stirs up anger. The tongue of the wise commends knowledge, but the mouths of fools pour out folly.

PROVERBS 15:4

A gentle tongue is a tree of life, but perverseness in it breaks the spirit.

PROVERBS 15:18

A hot-tempered man stirs up strife, but he who is slow to anger quiets contention.

PROVERBS 15:23

To make an apt answer is a joy to a man, and a word in season, how good it is!

PROVERBS 15:28

The heart of the righteous ponders how to answer, but the mouth of the wicked pours out evil things.

PROVERBS 16:13

Righteous lips are the delight of a king, and he loves him who speaks what is right.

PROVERBS 16:18

Pride goes before destruction, and a haughty spirit before a fall.

PROVERBS 16:23

The heart of the wise makes his speech judicious
and adds persuasiveness to his lips.

PROVERBS 16:24

Gracious words are like a honeycomb, sweetness to the soul and health to the body.

PROVERBS 16:27–28

A worthless man plots evil, and his speech is like a scorching fire. A dishonest man spreads strife, and a whisperer separates close friends.

PROVERBS 16:32

Whoever is slow to anger is better than the mighty, and he who rules his spirit than he who takes a city.

PROVERBS 17:10

A rebuke goes deeper into a man of understanding than a hundred blows into a fool.

PROVERBS 17:27–28

Whoever restrains his words has knowledge, and he who has a cool spirit is a man of understanding. Even a fool who keeps silent is considered wise; when he closes his lips, he is deemed intelligent.

PROVERBS 18:2

A fool takes no pleasure in understanding, but only in expressing his own opinion.

PROVERBS 18:4

The words of a man's mouth are deep waters; the fountain of wisdom is a bubbling brook.

PROVERBS 18:6–8

A fool's lips walk into a fight, and his mouth invites a beating. A fool's mouth is his ruin, and his lips are a snare to his soul. The words of a whisperer are like delicious morsels; they go down into the inner parts of the body.

PROVERBS 18:13

If one gives an answer before he hears, it is his folly and shame.

PROVERBS 18:17

The one who states his case first seems right, until the other comes and examines him.

PROVERBS 18:20–21

For the fruit of a man's mouth his stomach is satisfied; he is satisfied by the yield of his lips. Death and life are in the power of the tongue, and those who love it will eat its fruits.

PROVERBS 20:3
It is an honor for a man to keep aloof from strife, but every fool will be quarreling.

PROVERBS 21:23
Whoever keeps his mouth and his tongue keeps himself out of trouble.

PROVERBS 22:11
He who loves purity of heart, and whose speech is gracious, will have the king as his friend.

PROVERBS 25:11
A word fitly spoken is like apples of gold in a setting of silver.

PROVERBS 25:15
With patience a ruler may be persuaded,
and a soft tongue will break a bone.

PROVERBS 25:28
A man without self-control is like a city broken into and left without walls.

PROVERBS 26:4–5
Answer not a fool according to his folly, lest you be like him yourself. Answer a fool according to his folly, lest he be wise in his own eyes.

PROVERBS 26:18–19
Like a madman who throws firebrands, arrows, and death is the man who deceives his neighbor and says, I am only joking!

PROVERBS 26:20–22
For lack of wood the fire goes out, and where there is no whisperer, quarreling ceases. As charcoal to hot embers and wood to fire, so is a quarrelsome man for kindling strife. The words of a whisperer are like delicious morsels; they go down into the inner part of the body.

PROVERBS 26:23
Like the glaze covering an earthen vessel are fervent lips with an evil heart.

**PROVERBS 26:28**

A lying tongue hates its victims, and a flattering mouth works ruin.

**PROVERBS 27:2**

Let another praise you, and not your own mouth; a stranger and not your own lips.

**PROVERBS 27:5–6**

Better is open rebuke than hidden love. Faithful are the wounds of a friend; profuse are the kisses of an enemy.

**PROVERBS 29:11**

A fool gives full vent to his spirit, but a wise man quietly holds it back.

**PROVERBS 29:20**

Do you see a man who is hasty in his words? There is more hope for a fool than for him.

**ECCLESIASTES 5:2**

Be not rash with your mouth, nor let your heart be hasty to utter a word before God, for God is in heaven and you are on earth.

**ECCLESIASTES 10:12–14**

The words of a wise man's mouth win him favor, but the lips of a fool consume him. The beginning of the words of his mouth is foolishness, and the end of his talk is evil madness. A fool multiplies words, though no man knows what is to be, and who can tell him what will be after him?

**MATTHEW 7:1–5**

Judge not, that you be not judged. For with the judgment you pronounce you will be judged and with the measure you use it will be measured to you. Why do you see the speck that is in your brother's eye, but do not notice the log that is in your own eye? Or how can you say to your brother, "Let me take the speck out of your eye," when there is a log in your own eye? You hypocrite, first take the log out of your own eye, and then you will see clearly to take the speck out of your brother's eye.

MATTHEW 12:33–37

Either make the tree good and its fruit good; or make the tree bad and its fruit bad, for the tree is known by its fruit. You brood of vipers! How can you speak good, when you are evil? For out of the abundance of the heart the mouth speaks. The good person out of his good treasure brings forth good, and the evil person out of his evil treasure brings forth evil. If tell you, on the day of judgment, people will give account for every careless word they speak, for by your words you will be justified, and by your words you will be condemned.

EPHESIANS 4:29–30

Let no unwholesome talk come out of your mouth, but only as is good for building up, as fits the occasion, so that it might give grace to those who hear. And do not grieve the Holy Spirit of God, by whom you were sealed for the day of redemption.

EPHESIANS 4:31

Let all bitterness and wrath and anger and clamor and slander be put away from you, along with all malice.

COLOSSIANS 4:6

Let your speech always be gracious, seasoned with salt, so that you may know how you ought to answer each person.

2 TIMOTHY 2:24–25

And the Lord's servant must not be quarrelsome but kind to everyone, able to teach, patiently enduring evil, correcting his opponents with gentleness. God may perhaps grant them repentance that leads to a knowledge of the truth.

JAMES 1:19–21

Know this, my beloved brothers: let every person be quick to hear, slow to speak, slow to anger, for the anger of man does not produce the righteousness of God. Therefore, put away all filthiness and rampant wickedness and receive with meekness the implanted word which is able to save your souls.

JAMES 1:26
If anyone thinks he is religious and does not bridle his tongue but deceived his heart, this person's religion is worthless.

JAMES 3:1–12
Not many of you should become teachers, my brothers, for you know that we who teach will be judged with greater strictness. For we all stumble in many ways. And if anyone does not stumble in what he says, he is a perfect man, able also to bridle his whole body. If we put bits into the mouths of horses so that they obey us, we guide their whole bodies as well. Look at the ships also: though they are so large and are driven by strong winds, they are guided by a very small rudder wherever the will of the pilot directs. So also the tongue is a small member, yet hit boasts of great things.

How great a forest is set ablaze by such a small fire! And the tongue is a fire, a world of unrighteousness. The tongue is set among our members, staining the whole body, setting on fire the entire course of life, and set on fire by hell. For every kind of beast and bird, of reptile and sea creature, can be tamed and has been tamed by mankind, but no human being can tame the tongue. It is a restless evil, full of deadly poison. With it we bless our Lord and Father, and with it we curse people who are made in the likeness of God. From the same mouth come blessing and cursing. My brothers, these things ought not to be so. Does a spring pour forth from the same opening both fresh and salt water? Can a fig tree, my brothers, bear olives, or a grapevine produce figs? Neither can a salt pond yield fresh water.

JAMES 4:1–3
What causes quarrels and what causes fights among you? Is it not this, that your passions are at war within you? You desire and do not have, so you murder. You covet and cannot obtain, so you fight and quarrel. You do not have, because you do not ask. You ask and do not receive, because you ask wrongly, to spend it on your passions.

JAMES 4:11–12
Do not speak evil against one another, brothers. The one who speaks against a brother or judges his brother, speaks evil against the law and judges the law. But if you judge the law, you are not a doer of the law but a judge.

1 PETER 3:15

but in your hearts honor Christ the Lord as holy, always being prepared to make a defense to anyone who asks you for a reason for the hope that is in you; yet do it with gentleness and respect.

# 12 MARKS OF A QUARRELSOME TALKER[1]

## KEVIN DEYOUNG

Quarrels don't just happen. People make them happen.

Of course, there are honest disagreements and agree-to-disagree propositions, but that's not what the Bible means by quarreling. Quarrels, at least in Proverbs, are unnecessary arguments, the kind that honorable men stay away from (Prov. 17:14; 20:3). And elders too (1 Tim. 3). These fights aren't the product of a loving rebuke or a principled conviction. These quarrels arise because people are quarrelsome.

---

1. This was originally published on June 13, 2019, at The Gospel Coalition, https://www.thegospelcoalition.org/blogs/kevin-deyoung/distinguishing-marks-quarrelsome-person/

So what does a quarrelsome person look like? What are his (or her) distinguishing marks? Here are 12 possibilities.

You might be a quarrelsome person if:

1. *You defend every conviction with the same degree of intensity.* There are no secondary or tertiary issues. Everything is primary. You've never met a hill you wouldn't die on.

2. *You are quick to speak and slow to listen.* You rarely ask questions, and when you do it is to accuse or to continue prosecuting your case. You are not looking to learn, you are looking to defend, dominate, and destroy.

3. *Your only model for ministry and faithfulness is the showdown with the prophets of Baal on Mount Carmel.* Or the only Jesus you like is the Jesus who cleared the money-changers from the temple. Those are real examples in Scripture. But the Bible is a book, and sarcasm and whips are not the normal method of personal engagement.

4. *You are incapable of seeing nuances, and you do not believe in qualifying statements.* Everything in life is black and white without any gray.

5. *You never give the benefit of the doubt.* You do not try to read arguments in context. You put the worst possible construct on other's motives, and when there is a less flattering interpretation you go for that one.

6. *You have no unarticulated opinions.* Do people know what you think of everything? They shouldn't. That's why you have a journal or a prayer closet or a dog.

7. *You are unable to sympathize with your opponents.* You forget that sinners are also sufferers. You lose the ability to put yourself in someone else's shoes.

8. *Your first instinct is to criticize; your last instinct is to encourage.* Quarrelsome people almost always see others in need of rebuke, rarely in need of refreshing.

9. *You have a small grid, and everything fits in it.* You view life through a tiny prism such that you already know what everything is about. Everything is a social justice issue. Everything relates to the regulative principle. Everything

is Obama's fault. Everything is about Trump. It's all about the feminists. Or the patriarchy. Or how my parents messed up my life. When all you have is a hammer, the rest of the world looks like a nail.

10. *You derive a sense of satisfaction and spiritual safety in feeling constantly rejected.* We don't want to blame the victim, but some people are constitutionally unable to exist except as a remnant. They must be persecuted. They must be maligned. They do not know how to live in peacetime, only in war.

11. *You are always in the trenches with hand grenades strapped to your chest, never in the cafeteria with ice cream and ping pong.* I remember years ago talking to a returning serviceman in my church who told me sheepishly that his job in Iraq was to drive an armed convoy for the ice cream truck. It was extremely dangerous, escorting the vehicle through bomb infested territory. This was brave, honorable work. And important: even soldiers need ice cream once in a while. The amp doesn't have to be cranked to 11 all the time. Seriousness about God is not the same as pathological seriousness about everything. Remember G. K. Chesterton: "We have to feel the universe at once as an ogre's castle, to be stormed, and yet as our own cottage, to which we can return to at evening."

12. *You have never changed your mind.* If you haven't changed your mind on an important matter in several presidents, I wonder if you are a Christian or even alive. Of course, truth never changes, and neither should many of our convictions. But quarrelsome people stir up strife because, already knowing everything, they have no need to listen, learn, or ask questions.

## DIRECT HIT?

Hit close to home? Look to Christ. He has the power to change us and has made provision to forgive. By the death of the Prince of Peace we can be at peace with God and at peace with one another.

**TGC** | THE GOSPEL COALITION

The Gospel Coalition (TGC) supports the church in making disciples of all nations, by providing gospel-centered resources that are trusted and timely, winsome and wise.

Guided by a Council of more than 40 pastors in the Reformed tradition, TGC seeks to advance gospel-centered ministry for the next generation by producing content (including articles, podcasts, videos, courses, and books) and convening leaders (including conferences, virtual events, training, and regional chapters).

In all of this we want to help Christians around the world better grasp the gospel of Jesus Christ and apply it to all of life in the 21st century. We want to offer biblical truth in an era of great confusion. We want to offer gospel-centered hope for the searching.

Join us by visiting TGC.org so you can be equipped to love God with all your heart, soul, mind, and strength, and to love your neighbor as yourself.